821
Langland

Ryan, W
William Langland

cop.a

495

DEC 1 1 1960

821
Langland

Ryan, W
William Langland

cop.a

495

SAN DIEGO PUBLIC LIBRARY

LIBRARY RULES

TIME: — Books may be kept 14 days, unless dated otherwise.

RENEWALS: — Books may be renewed once at the agency where borrowed, unless on reserve. Bring book with you.

FINES: — Five cents a day will be charged for each book kept overtime.

DAMAGES: — *Injury to the book from tearing, penciling, unusual soiling or other ill-usage, will be charged to the card owner. Please report to us when a mutilated book is issued to you.*

CARDS—ALWAYS BRING YOUR CARD WITH YOU.

Twayne's English Authors Series

Sylvia E. Bowman, *Editor*

INDIANA UNIVERSITY

William Langland

William Langland

By WILLIAM M. RYAN

University of Missouri at Kansas City

Twayne Publishers, Inc.   ::   New York

To Fay

Preface

IN 1958, when I made the first step toward this study of William Langland's fourteenth-century poem *Piers Plowman* (*The Vision of William Concerning Piers Plowman*), a number of now-established books and essays by editors and critics had yet to appear. There has been, in fact, a recent increase in activity in the broad area of *Piers Plowman* criticism, and I have little confidence that any remarks of mine concerning allegory or general schema or bi-directional lines of influence might add perceptibly to the swelling harvest.

My recourse is, instead, ". . . to go and glene after" (C IX, 67). Keeping in mind the student and general reader, I have sought the man Langland, a poet of whom there is much to be said, and I have highlighted the features of *Piers Plowman* which I believe to be of most use to the beginner. This book is, therefore, more literal than might be expected by experienced students of medieval poetry; it is weighted with the solid stuff of characterization, word-play, metrics, social satire, and such specifics as the Seven Deadly Sins. Religious allegory is taken at surface level for the most part, and students of theology will gain more from my references to the authorities than from my occasional and general comments on doctrinal problems and Langland's concept of salvation.

Because I am convinced that it is in his re-tellings that Langland reveals most about himself, I have made use of all three of the texts of *Piers Plowman*. Copious citations are presented in order to impress upon the reader Langland's fondness for word-play, his changing attitudes as he worked through the two revisions, and even the possibility that his spiritual expansion kept pace with the years. My approach requires some patience in the reader, for he is expected to digest tables of line numbers, word-lists, and partial collations as clues in the search. This fare may grow uncomfortably concentrated at times, but the statistical nature of such evidence leaves no alternative. Perhaps my speculations, although they are based on the outdated edition of the B and C versions, will help to open some part of the branching road that lies ahead.

To Professor Rudolph Willard I wish once again to express my gratitude for counsels of the duties of scholarship—heights I have yet to scale. In the present instance he has facilitated my work by the loan of his copies of the Vercelli Book and of Bodleian Manuscripts Junius 85 and 86. I am indebted to British librarians for granting me the privilege of reading in collections of manuscripts containing Old English homilies: Dr. R. W. Hunt, the Bodleian Library; Dr. C. E. Wright, the British Museum Manuscript Room; Dr. Richard Vaughan, Corpus Christi College Library, Cambridge. Professor Archibald A. Hill, editor of *Studies in Honor of Rudolph Willard* (University of Texas Press, 1968), kindly permitted the use of portions of my article "Word-play in Some Old English Homilies and a Late Middle-English Poem." All quotations from *Piers Plowman* are taken from the W. W. Skeat edition of the three texts of *Piers Plowman.* This edition and Dorothy Bethurum's edition of Wulfstan (*The Homilies of Wulfstan*) were used by permission of the Clarendon Press, Oxford. The reproduced folio on the dust jacket was provided by the Pierpont Morgan Library, owner of an early fifteenth-century manuscript of *Piers Plowman.* Professor Sylvia E. Bowman gave the manuscript a reading so close as to repair its style and so pellucid in perspective as to regiment its order.

Financial assistance which expedited the completion of this book was provided by the Kansas City Association of Trusts and Foundations and the University of Kansas City (now the University of Missouri at Kansas City).

Miss Jenny Stigers was stoical in her typing of the manuscript.

WILLIAM M. RYAN

University of Missouri—Kansas City

Contents

Contents

Chronology

The name "William Langland" is the only biographical datum of which we have any certainty. All other items pertaining to Langland's life are possibilities, with the evidence weighing more in their favor than against; and all dates are approximate.

1332   William Langland is born at Cleobury Mortimer in Shropshire County in West England, the son of Stacy de Rokayle.

1352   He is given a formal education and takes Minor Orders, which he holds for the remainder of his life.

1362   Moves to London and settles in Cornhill with his wife, Kitte, and his daughter, Kalote.

1370   A text of *Piers Plowman*.

1377   B text of *Piers Plowman*.

1392   C text of *Piers Plowman*.

1400   Death of William Langland.

The dates of various literary and historical events which probably fall within the lifetime of William Langland are of some help in placing him in his period.

1371   John of Gaunt begins his rise to power.

1372–   Chaucer's *The House of Fame*.
1380

1375–   The Pearl Poet's *Sir Gawain and the Green Knight*.
1400

1376   Pestilence.

1377   Death of King Edward III; accession of King Richard II.

1377–   Wyclif translates the Bible.
1379

1378   The Great Schism (Pope Urban VI vs. Anti-Pope Clement VII).

1379   Introduction of the hated poll tax.

1380–   Chaucer's *Troilus and Criseyde; Parliament of Fowls*.
1386

1381 Peasants' Revolt, also called Wat Tyler's Rebellion.
1384 Death of Wyclif.
1387– Chaucer's *The Canterbury Tales*.
1400
1390 The Pearl Poet's *The Pearl*. John Gower's *Confessio Aman-tis*.
1392 Truce with the French. Generally improved conditions.
1399 Accession of King Henry IV.
1400 Death of Geoffrey Chaucer.

CHAPTER 1

The Search

NO other Middle English allegory of homiletic character approaches *Piers Plowman* in quality, scope, and complexity. In all of medieval religious literature, for that matter, only *The Divine Comedy* of Dante stands above it. The great English poem raises its odd and wondrous form at some distance from the lesser works of uniform design; it is as much alone as its maker must have been—Will Langland, a poor cleric sadly miscast in a life of indignity and penury.

The poem's uniqueness is an enticement to the inquisitive student, who should not be put off by its reputation for difficulty. There will be no extraordinary call upon his patience—little more, for reasons of vocabulary and orthography, than in the reading of Chaucer[1] and Gower, probably less than in the elegy *The Pearl* and the romances *Sir Gawain and the Green Knight* and The Alliterative *Morte Arthure*, all of which, like *Piers Plowman*, contain attitudes, allusions, and details which are characteristically medieval. Langland, moreover, had a general audience in mind. In making its appeal to two or more levels of society, *Piers Plowman* is to be distinguished from all other long and ambitious works of the period except *Cursor Mundi*.

Piers Plowman is also unusual in its incorporation of some of the main features of three distinct types of literature: Anglo-Saxon verse (line structure of *Piers Plowman* approximates that of the long alliterative line); allegorical drama; and prose homily[2] (these latter two overlap in their didactic elements, which *Piers Plowman* shares).[3] Like the drama, *Piers Plowman* has a complete cast of brilliantly sketched symbolic allegorical figures; a plot and subplot that have dramatic highlights; and a steady progression of events. As regards the homily, there are lessons from Scripture with interpretative remarks by the author; and the entire poem is a lesson.

I *The Poet*

A strong inducement to the reader is the possibly factual autobiographical data on Langland,[4] for the like of whom, as a writing eccentric, we can at most compare John Bunyan, Samuel Butler, and Laurence Sterne. These data are few and questionable,
however, and the man and his manners can best be visualized by
those willing to depend, not upon what his contemporaries recorded about him, for that has been lost, nor upon a few seeming
references to himself, but rather upon the content, style, and attitudes of the poem. I shall attempt to show that in the individual
lines there is a surprisingly high yield of aspects of the author's
personality. Even his name, for which the evidence in public
records is very dubious, is possibly still to be found.[5] In other passages (C VI, 2: XXI, 473) mention is made of his wife and daughter, whom we are free to view either as mere fictions or, particularly if we accept the hypothesis that Langland held only minor
orders, as his real-life family. Somehow the latter view is more
impressive, for Langland seems altogether too preoccupied with
poverty to be a celibate living "out of the world."

Patient poverty, his most constant theme, is, after charity, a
noble condition and a virtue in itself. But it is impatient poverty
that often raises its plaintive voice in *Piers Plowman;* and, far
from the true friar's or anchorite's relish for the pinched and stale
drabness of the poor, Langland feels the righteous and, in a way,
amusing indignation of the harassed husband and father who
never manages to make ends meet. He speaks of going about "in
manere of a mendynaunt" (mendicant) (B XIII, 3); and the
phrase "wete-shoed" is often on his mind (B XIV, 161; XVIII, 1).
References to cold and hunger are too numerous to be listed, but
later, in Chapter 3, we discuss *rich* and *poor.*

The reader of *Piers Plowman* can quite easily picture a tall, lean
figure (like Virgil), nervous in his movements, taut with sup-
pressed energy, yet physically futile—all in all rather a helpless
creature as he forced himself to go his rounds of praying, psalm-
singing, and lesson-reading so that he might have assurance of an
evening meal and some provision for his dependents. But, however inept he may have proved himself as ecclesiastical careerist
and as head of a family, however frustrated he may have been in
his lowly station and duties of this life, and however discouraged

and even humiliated he was at a given time, he must have borne with him the sweet and heavy burden of his mission as an artist; he must have known that to hold his little troubles against the broad ground of Piers the plowman was to conjure them away.

One of the pieces in the puzzle, one of Langland's paradoxes, is that, for a man of his intellectual potential, he settled for very little—no fame nor fortune was his, not even that blessing of most clerics, security. He tells us of Will's (and possibly his own) aversion for physical labor: "Ich am to waik to worche with sykel other with sythe, / And to long, leyf [believe] me, lowe for to stoupe" (C VI, 23–24); Sloth also says, "I may nouȝte stonde ne stoupe . . ." (B V, 394). Obviously, Langland rationalizes his physical laziness and makes a joke at his own expense. Coupled with this characteristic is what has been called "Will's human sloth, his shrinking from *spiritual* labor" [6] (italics mine). Surely with his gifts, if Langland had really striven in the church, he would have helped himself as well as others and thereby would have alleviated the bitterness that sets his satire apart from that of Chaucer.

Intellectually, Langland also appears to have been unambitious —or is it possible that his humility was such that intellectual striving or even achievements would be repellent to him? In this connection it must be noted that there are several anti-intellectual passages in the poem. He had before him the example of monk-scholars whose humility was unquestionable; at the same time, he knew the history of the Schoolmen, their acrimonious disputes, their exalted postures. Like Chaucer and Sir Philip Sidney, he has never a syllable of self-praise. Whatever the answer may be, he downgraded pretentious learning, hinted that he found physical labor inordinately difficult, and resigned himself as a minor cleric to routine chores that demanded little of him.

He sounds like a man bound for failure, but in his occupation as a poet he showed an entirely different self to the world. From his thirties through his sixties he kept at one job, the writing of a single poem. The labor was long, and it was fed by thoughts that were longer. Unique in countless ways, *Piers Plowman* is Langland's only known work. No one in the history of English literature has produced as his sole masterpiece a poem of equal magnitude. If Langland had entirely kept subjectivity out of his poetry, thereby precluding all biographical speculations, it would still be possible to envision a giant of a poet who lived in the shadows and never digressed from a single, obsessive goal—a poem which would be epic in length and breadth, take full account of the human comedy, and instruct with Christlike compassion and solicitude all the wayward folk inhabiting the fair fields of this world.

"Giant," a term which Langland used and understood in its full, traditional sense, may seem a strange one to apply to the all but anonymous author of a poem which has in modern times come in for a surprising amount of abuse, considering the smallness of its audience. However, as a Middle English poem it has also received —particularly during the past forty years—critical treatment both fair and appreciative that is second in volume only to the great body of Chaucer criticism. Langland is also second to Chaucer as a source of influence emanating from the late fourteenth century throughout the fifteenth and sixteenth centuries.[7] He stands with Dante and Chaucer, the two other medieval writers who were conceivers of projects far beyond the range of normal vision.

All English writers with grand visions, except Langland and Bunyan, during long and productive lives, multiplied their works with the benefit of advice and stimulation from the finest minds and talents of their day. To Langland, the courts of the mighty lords of state and church were an utterly unattainable world, and he was never to know anything like Chaucer's easy intercourse with the intelligentsia of England and France. Had he lived two centuries later, Langland might have found a welcome at the Mermaid Tavern, the Devil, or the Half Moon, to name a few at random; but the London of his day would seldom have afforded him opportunity to make poet's talk with his own breed. There is no indication that his many years in London brought him any closer at the end than at the beginning to the milieu in which he rightly belonged, nor any indication that, in spite of the accepted value of his sermon-in-verse and its success in reaching the common people, he was sustained or so much as encouraged by a patron.

II *Complexity*

There are additional reasons for putting in a class by himself this solitary poet who conceived, probably without being entirely aware that he was doing so, a single plan for his entire life. Again, the size and complexity of his canvas remind us of Dante's, and he has, in fact, frequently been compared with the Italian poet.[8] It is difficult to make one's way through *The Divine Comedy,* and even more so to give *Piers Plowman* an exhaustive reading. Furthermore, having got to the end of either, the reader must retrace and reconsider, finding new insights in light of his acquaintance with the whole, and even then his retention of the whole will not be perfect.

There are many English writers whose tendency is obscurantist because they sacrifice immediate communication for ultimate communication through ambiguities. Examples are Jonathan Swift's *The Tale of a Tub,* notorious in graduate seminars, and Thomas Carlyle's *Sartor Resartus* which, in the whole cloth, tends to suffocate. In the realm of poetry, obscurity may result from any one of a number of causes and usually does result from a single cause in a given poem. The use of allegory in *The Pearl* leaves questions unanswered today; it is also allegory, as would be expected, that impedes the modern reader of *Pilgrim's Progress.* Some of the subtleties of *Piers Plowman* must have presented a stiff challenge even to Langland's contemporaries; and modern interpreters of Langland, who would take everything the poet offers, must constantly be prepared to come to a dead stop and to winnow one line patiently until its hidden meaning falls clear.[9]

Downright vagueness is another cause of obscurity in some poetry, as, for example, the philosophizing in Robert Browning.[10] Langland, too, is vague at times, and not only when he is projecting an idea with personifications. He is indefinite when he talks about London, though he ordinarily provides solidly literal details on other subjects. In certain lines containing phrases of a puzzling nature, the key to Langland's choice of words lies in word-play, which is discussed in Chapter 6.

The one cause of obscurity that is most familiar in modern poetry—extreme privateness of allusion (James Joyce, T. S. Eliot, Dylan Thomas, *et al.*)—scarcely blurs a line of *Piers Plowman.* In a few places Langland may be telling more than we read, but his subjectivity is, for the most part, a matter of emotion or opinion rather than of allusive detail. Scholars have long tried, and long will try, no doubt, to determine where or how Langland learned so much about the law, whether he actually was a married man or merely cast himself as one while he played the Dreamer, and whether he was always indigent or had traveled abroad and had friends in high places. David C. Fowler, in a departure from all other members of the present generation of *Piers Plowman* critics, argues with impressive resourcefulness but insufficient proof that John of Trevisa wrote the B text.[11]

Fortunately for us moderns the few remote details that are possibly moored to some fourteenth-century reality are not of key importance to the poem; an exact location "on Maluerne hulles" is not the focal point of Passus I, nor Meed's real-life model of Passus II. Any stream will serve in descriptive passages; any ale-wife and any low tavern will accommodate the glutton.

Piers Plowman is, then, a poem typical in its occasional obscurities, none of which loom high as obstacles to the reader. In the main a work of directness and literalness, it requires of the modern reader, not that he turn with every line to commentary and gloss, but rather that he open his mind to questions of faith and morals and that he look for universals in Langland's characters, themes, and artistic devices. With no intention of detracting from the importance, which is very great, of the scores of critical studies—both books and articles—which have anatomized the great poem bit by bit as an exemplar of medieval sermon, medieval allegory, medieval pamphlet, medieval creed, I hope in the present study to treat *Piers Plowman* as a work of timeless appeal built on verses of dazzling variety. I shall try to show that the verses are charged and colored like Chaucer's and Shakespeare's and Milton's with the maker's personality. Verse of this order has always stood the gaze of strangers from another age, and predictably *Piers Plowman* will hold its position in English letters for as long a time as civilized men are interested in tradition and, in this particular case, immortality.

III *Piers*

Probably the most conspicuous matter for speculation in the poem is the character Piers himself. Langland's choice of a plowman presents no mystery, though to a modern reader it may seem a matter of indifference whether the common-man protagonist is plowman or shepherd. Langland lumps together "plowmen and pastoures and pore comune laborers. / Souteres [cobblers] and shepherdes. . . ." (B X, 459–60); and he includes the entire working class in the person of the humble plowman.

Until farm work was depersonalized in our age of automation, the man behind the plow was for us, as he still is for most of the world, a symbol of productive labor. He must be a strong man if the furrows are to be straight and deep. He makes visible progress by the minute, and there is no turning back or even looking back. He strides and scrambles, hops and stumbles; but he follows that plow and keeps his weight on it, with his eyes fixed straight ahead to the distant point and his hands gripped tightly on the handles. Langland's plowman, a guide to the rest of humanity, is an embodiment of what R. W. Frank, Jr., has called "The Scheme of Salvation." [12] For Langland's view of a direct route to heaven, Piers the plowman is a more inspiring symbol than Bunyan's pilgrim, who is often misled.

Langland was not the first to discover the allegorical uses of the plowman,[13] but it should be safe to say that Langland's is the best accommodation of the figure. In addition to the theme of salvation, there is the element of humility which must have entered into the decision to accept that tried and proven archetype of simple worthiness, the plowman. We have noted Langland's abstention from self-praise and the adjustment of this remarkable man to a mean existence. However the psychologists may explain lack of ambition, it must be true that humility is one factor. Moreover, in the mind of a man who has been a watchful observer of the cheats (*losengeres*), flatterers, and impostors (*faitoures*) who make their way to the top, it undoubtedly seemed that most of Christ's own children were to be found among the little people who hoped for no more than a full belly and a place of shelter.

Langland might have chosen a ruler, steering not a plow but the great ship of state, or any noble lord (as, for example, the familiar prince of the highly secularized courtesy books of a century and a half later). He might have chosen a prelate, who could look down from his eminence on the fair field full of folk as Dante and Virgil, Dante's guide, look on from points of detachment. The father-narrator in *The Pearl* views the heavenly throng from his side of the river. In *Paradise Lost,* God the Father and His Son have earth under their surveillance. But then there is Chaucer, shuffling around unobtrusively among the other pilgrims. In this, as in many other matters, Langland's affinity is with his contemporary.

Piers is not the only observer of people acting out their parts in Langland's poem. He does not, in fact, even appear until Passus

VIII (C), when he "putte forth hus hefd." [14] Throughout the first
seven passus we have been watching the King and Meed and numerous other allegorical characters through the eyes of the
Dreamer who, again, is one of the crowd, an inconspicuous foot-
traveler dressed as a hermit. The convention of the dream-vision is
an old and familiar one in Langland's time, but what is not so
common is the dreamer's relegation of himself to a humble place
in the society he describes.

Langland is, then, using himself as an example of humility, to
him one of the most important virtues. Humility is a major motif
in the poem; and, since its practice precludes self-love, it does
bear directly upon his central message of love for one's fellow
man—just as love was Christ's message and, in our own time, was
the beginning and the end of all of human existence in the mind of
Pope John XXIII. Salvation is man's goal, and *Piers Plowman,* as
an exhaustive treatise on the means of salvation for the layman
active in the world, defines love from every relevant approach
(without, incidentally, ever setting foot in the pavilions of romance).

Much of Langland's argument has to do with the threat of
doom through failure of charity; and the dark side of his picture—
particularly the first of the two main divisions of the poem, the
Visio—presents also exhaustively and in great detail the means
whereby man can live falsely; follow Lady Meed, who is greed;
and lose the heavenly kingdom. Here Langland parades before us
in scenes of vivid, tangible realism the worst sources of temptation
—all the deadly sins which human flesh and frailty are prone to
commit. Avarice is the sin for which Langland seems to reproach
himself most often, and it also heads the list of seven as he orders
it.

But how could he have chosen otherwise when his theme is
charity, and he would teach by contrast that, while giving of oneself is the key to salvation, self-seeking is the key to condemnation? Even more appropriately than anger does avarice match
against love. The Ten Commandments specify killing, but not the
emotional response-without-action which is anger. Both the Old
and New Testaments vindicate righteous anger, and although the
Scholastics and modern theologians alike have much to say about
the propriety of obtaining material goods necessary to a normal
secular life—such acquisition being merely an extension of the

struggle to survive—no one has ever tried to describe a righteous avarice. Coveting of neighbor's goods and gathering of luxurious ones stem the flow of charity, causing it not to begin at home but to fail even to be conceived. "Waster" is to Langland a stronger term than his anonymous predecessor by a few years made of it in *Wynnere and Wastour*.[15]

To remind men to love one another is, therefore, the aim of the poem. Langland knew charity to be a tenuous and imperiled element in his society; he was sickened by the cruelty and selfishness of his fellow creatures. Since he himself desired to do better, and since this involved increased generosity, it was natural that he should share as fully as possible the formula which he and his church believed to be the best one for right living. That he succeeded in his desire to share the truths he had learned is attested to by the number of extant manuscript copies of *Piers Plowman*—there are over fifty.

The mystery surrounding the progressively changing character named Piers Plowman will not be cleared away in the present study. R. W. Frank, Jr., building on an earlier theory of Konrad Burdach's, believes it possible that a Piers Plowman familiar to fourteenth-century Englishmen was understood to be both human and semidivine and that Langland's Piers would, therefore, be accepted with a minimum of explanation—which is certainly all that Langland can be said to provide.[16] Readers today will have to leave this theory untested, but of one thing they can be certain. Piers Plowman is an idealized character from start to finish—as a common plowman, he is the best of all plowmen and consequently is sufficiently respected by people of his class that they look to him for guidance. Later it is Piers for whom Truth sends, bidding him plow the earth. Truth presents Piers with a pardon for him and his heirs (followers) forever.

In the last stage of Piers' development, he is identified with Christ; we may as well say that Piers *is* Christ. Although in the main Langland's allegory is of the simplest variety—on two levels and no more—ambiguities now open out in more than two directions.[17] *Petrus, id est Christus* seems plain enough. But the apostle Peter was not Christ; he was Christ's vicar; the Incarnation was not followed by a reincarnation. Piers, another spelling for *Petrus*, is helping to lead his people toward eternal salvation; he is doing Christ's work, as a cleric in his time was expected to do; but Piers

is a layman and his activities are beyond the periphery where
Langland himself was authorized to work. Langland would have
before his mind's eye the picture of the anguished Christ in Geth-
semane submitting to divine law, thus extending love of law to the
last degree.

To take another approach, however, there is the possibility of a
miraculous transformation. This event would require a drastic revision of the Christ legend, and in the revision a simple plowman
would have such access of divine grace that he would be trans-
formed into the Son of God. The only parallel would be the life of
Mary herself; and then the marvelous transformation undergone
at the time of her pregnancy, when she became the mother of
God, would have to be compared with the infinitely more marvelous deification of carnate man. For a (so far as we know) completely orthodox William Langland, this idea would have been
unthinkable. He may, nevertheless, have projected in his idealiza-
tion of the plowman a gradual ascending through the upper levels
of the great chain of being until Piers arrived at a condition in
which his relationship to his fellow humans would be Christlike.[18]
Petrus then would mean "like Christ," an epithet which history
has reserved for only a few.

Or the poem's purpose may be by use of myth, in the fashion of
the *Odyssey*, or fiction like Kazantzakis' St. Francis of Assisi (who
was Christlike), to create a latter-day apparition of Christ in the
guise of a plowman in England of the third quarter of the fourteenth century. The Incarnation, which John Lawlor calls "Langland's central doctrine," would, in a purely imaginary way, be
presented as the process in which there occurred the dual phe-
nomena of God-made-man, man-made-God. Whatever the intended relationship between God and His creature, and regardless of the nature of the change of identity which takes place in
the poem, Langland shows us that the best of men become God-
like through good works and that the Incarnation, by no means a
device that ushers all souls into heaven, supplies the faithful with
an *immediate* inspiration to carry on in the struggle. The prospect
of eternal bliss is the greatest inspiration conceivable, but it requires that attention be directed a long distance away, to a point
beyond the universe. Christ comes only once into the here and
now, briefly; and after Him come the good priests of whom Piers,
though he is not specifically so styled, is one. He helps men to find

Truth and teaches them how to serve her and, through obedience to law, how to serve each other.

IV *The Texts*

Piers Plowman is not read at a sitting. Like Edmund Spenser's *The Faerie Queene* and Robert Burton's *The Anatomy of Melancholy*, it has probably been read in its entirety by only a small percentage of its admiring public. Since the "entirety" of this poem includes three versions, now and forever to be known as A, B, and C, and since the only way to get at all three, for the present and for the next few years to come, is to read the eighty-year-old edition of W. W. Skeat (six hundred pages plus a volume of notes and glossary), it is to be expected that only specializing students will digest all of it.[19]

Each of the three texts is an entity; and, if the poem survived in only one of the three, it would still stand second only to *The Canterbury Tales* as a Middle English poem. It may be recommended that students should read the B version if expediency is sought. However, if two of the versions are passed over, much of importance is missed: the shifts in the poet's personal esthetic, in depths of conviction, and in values in general; and especially the increase in his spirituality and humanity.

Line by line comparison of A, B, and C is a rather laborious task; the more pleasant chore of reading the three versions in order, straight through, will at least leave general impressions of growth and change, and these will afford the rare opportunity to look into the secrets of an artist's inner life as his work reveals it. It is, in fact, a unique opportunity; for, while other poets were productive over periods of long duration, no major poet has confined himself for so many years to continuous revision of a single poem. Taking a long view, it can be said that the poem tells as much about Langland as it does its own story.

And *Piers Plowman* must be read in Middle English.[20] Although Langland has not Chaucer's polish and capacity for epigrammatizing, it may be said that *Piers Plowman* in certain respects demands preservation of its Middle English form even more emphatically than do the works of Chaucer. The principal reason is the obvious one that is germane also to Anglo-Saxon verse: the long alliterative line with its four primary stresses (normally three alliterations) is simply not convertible into any of the forms of

modern English verse. At least it can be said for the modernizing
of Chaucer that couplets in iambic pentameter are as much *au
courant* today as they were in Chaucer's own time though they are
not, to be sure, to be compared in popularity with the same form
in its heyday, the eighteenth century.

Fortunately studies are available in print which interpret Langland's revisions from various points of view for the serious student
who willingly reads through to the end of the C text but has not
sufficient time or motivation to make a microscopic cross-analysis.
E. T. Donaldson's book,[21] by far the most insightful critique of this
type, rightly concentrates on the poet as he neared the end of his
labors in the C text. In Chapter 3 I offer the results of my collation
of the three texts with full realization that my dependence on
Skeat's edition precludes the reaching of conclusions and possibly
disqualifies some of my "findings." At the same time, since such
analysis is so long overdue, it can be argued that, where the patterns of Langland's ideas and attitudes come through strongly
with numerous citations behind them, these patterns merit attention for the time being; indeed, some of them invite speculation.
Until all three texts are published, the only other way to proceed
is out of the question—to collate all manuscripts as part of the
groundwork for a definitive study.

Synopsis of the three texts would be of little or no value in this
project. The poem is crowded with a cast of over one hundred
and forty characters and a vast accumulation of concrete and ab-
stract details. And the plot, if it may be so called, is divided into
eleven visions as well as into two main parts: the Visio of the
narrator turned hermit and the Vita, which is in three parts—the
Vita de Dowel, Vita de Dobet, and Vita de Dobest. There are
other complications. In the Vita de Dowel the very important
character Activa Vita—also called Haukyn the active man, sinful
but redeemable—plays a role that exemplifies one element in the
way of life that must be followed from Dowel through Dobet to
Dobest. With Langland's often demonstrated sympathy for the
common man—the laborer—the term Active Life, or Active Man,
would seem to be self-explanatory; and to a certain extent it is.
But activity cannot stop with the meeting of the responsibility of
earning a living, and so the term, like everything else in this allegory, is ambiguous. It pertains to prayer in all its forms, of which
the first and foremost is obedience to the law, which, like every-

thing man does that brings him closer to salvation, is a form of prayer. If obedience fails, the prayer of repentance must follow. (Haukyn repents sincerely.)

Activa Vita is an underlying element in the Vita division of the poem and must not be correlated with Dowel, Dobet, and Dobest. In comparison with them, Haukyn is a prisoner; the marketplace is his prison; and, for all its ambivalence and its undenied prominence in Langland's scheme, Activa Vita is subsidiary to the three vitas. These represent the totality of human existence on an idealized plane where all the problems found in the Visio have been overcome, and Piers, the good man, is seen advancing through ever higher stages toward his ultimate union with divinity. Piers must live through each in turn; he is not, however, the Active Man himself but he does perform as guide and teacher. A real hermit—not the one Langland portrays as mingling among all the classes of people at the beginning of the poem—of strict contemplative rule could earn eternal happiness in *his* way. A good king—an energetic but elevated being—may likewise be saved. Activa Vita is simply Langland's description of the average man; and Langland, as socially responsible a poet as ever lived, tailors his poem to fit all those who must toil for their daily bread, thus concerning himself with the largest possible segment of society.

Further complication results from the interweaving of Visio and Vita, with continuation of the occurrence of visions after the poet has left the Visio and entered the Vita. There is also a kind of vita in the Visio that is personified in a character named Do-evil who is not developed, is in fact barely mentioned. Both of the two mentions are merely brief reminders of another way of life that is alien to right-living society as Langland conceives it. Within Do-evil, an almost pure abstraction as are Dowel, -bet, and -best, there are incorporated such characters as False, Favel (Flattery), Simony; Liar, Guile, as well as the Seven Deadly Sins! Similarly, when Lady Holychurch directs the Dreamer to look on his "left halfe"—if he would see "the false" whom she calls False, Favel, and Liar—the Dreamer sees only Lady Meed. False and Favel are, therefore, the same.

The above indications of Langland's penchant for shifting his ground without warning are only a few of the many possible examples, but they should suffice as proof of the difficulties awaiting the would-be synopsizer of the poem. The most extensive interpretative summary to date is that of John Lawlor in *Piers Plowman: An Essay in Criticism*. Even in 167 pages—and nothing less could do justice to *Piers Plowman*—Lawlor's retelling is necessarily omissive in certain parts; and, except for a few cross references to the C text, he makes no attempt to compare the three texts.

CHAPTER 2

A, B, and C as a Possible Key

NEXT to nothing is known about the life of the fourteenth-century British citizen who probably went by the name of William Langland. A search of the past six hundred years of English literature yields no other major writer on whom there is so little definite biographical data. However, it is true that, in Langland's own time and within his own school (consisting of the Northern poets of the alliterative revival), there were a number of poets of undeniable greatness whose names, like most names before 1500, were lost to manuscript copyists within a short time of the composition of their works. The master elegist (of *The Pearl*) and master of romance who wrote *Sir Gawain and the Green Knight,* and the great mystic who brought forth *The Cloud of the Unknowing* are not only anonymous but, in contrast to the sometimes autobiographic Langland, are submerged from view in their works. On the other hand there is Chaucer, who does reveal what seem to be facts of personality, experience, and physique and about whom the life records promise to produce an unparalleled (for a medieval writer) abundance of additional facts. Already we have a substantial beginning toward a life of Chaucer.[1]

I *Biographical Studies*

Langland's biography is another story—if there is one at all. Lack of proof of formal education, obscurity of his career, and even his possible illegitimacy[2] would seem to remove any likelihood that investigation, however thoroughgoing, of church and public records will turn up significant new data concerning his life. The few clues contained within the lines of *Piers Plowman* have been, one would think, just about exhausted by generations of scholars eager to construct some outline of the man behind the poem; and critical studies of *Piers Plowman* more often than not have included brief quasi-biographical sketches based on what

Langland says, or seems to say, about his chosen work, his ideal-
ism, his poverty, his unsuitability to manual labor, his wife and
children, and so forth. Skeat showed the way, and others followed
with interpretations pointing toward definition of Langland's image; and it is cause for joy that this image is emerging year by
year under the present steady floodlighting of the poem by American and British medievalists. An example, in connection with the
question of Langland's education, is Morton Bloomfield's argument that it is not implausible that Langland was educated in an
English university, possibly a Benedictine College at Oxford.[3]

The principal deterrent to further construction of the poet's real-
life image has been and still is the lack of an ABC edition complete with variant readings from all the manuscripts. George
Kane's edition of the A text is the first step in this gigantic task.
Skeat's edition, monumental and indispensable for most of a century, did not evaluate the manuscripts with perfect accuracy;
moreover, not all of the manuscripts known to us today were
available at the time Skeat was working. Until the long-awaited
and happy date when Kane and E. T. Donaldson will bring out
the B text and A. G. Mitchell and G. H. Russell the C text, a
definitive analysis of the poem cannot be made.[4] Contained as it
is in three versions, *Piers Plowman* presents complexities and difficulties to the textual critic which would be formidable enough if
in some hard-to-imagine white heat of creativity the poet had
made all three versions within a year or two. At least he would be
the same man, slightly older, much fatigued, but not noticeably
altered in his philosophy of life and his approach to his art. The C
version, or whatever his editors might have decided to call the
final version of this accelerated revision would, one should guess,
be the best; and acceptance of it would be according to the usual
practice of taking the writer's word that "Here, I place in your
hands the last draft of my work. It's the best I can do with it." In
the case of a medieval writer, our main problem would then be
evaluation and collation of extant manuscripts of the poem in its
perfected form.

II   *Three Versions*

No such simple solution exists for the student of *Piers Plowman*.
In my discussion of its uniqueness as the sole product of Langland's poetic career, I touched on the long duration of the project.

At one extreme the poem is said to have been written over a period from 1360 to 1400. An estimate no doubt much nearer the fact, but probably too conservative, restricts all three versions to a ten-year period, 1370 to 1380. A reasonable compromise that is historically defensible would extend Langland's work on the poem over a period of approximately twenty years, from 1370 to 1390. We are quite certain that the B version was written in 1377.

Each of the three versions has its own peculiar features of style and content, and the attitudes of the poet, as he progressed from youth to middle to old age, change remarkably. To bring more boldly into view than has been done heretofore some of the more significant changes is one of the major objectives of the present study. It is undeniable that a thoroughly sound comparison of the three texts cannot be made until such time as they and all of the necessary apparatus are conveniently at hand in the new editions, for only then will the extent of scribal interference be determinable. Notwithstanding the often-voiced argument of enforced delay, a number of critics from Skeat on down to E. T. Donaldson have formed opinions regarding the so-called "C" poet as distinguished from the "A" and "B" poets.

Donaldson has not only made the major contribution of an entire book on the C text but has also addressed himself particularly to the traits of the poet in his last period. He finds the "C" poet more active in revising than "B," but "C" sometimes lacks inspiration and repeats himself as a consequence.[5] Donaldson makes a questionable statement when he says that "In more than 99 per cent of their seven-thousand-odd lines there is little to choose between B and C."[6] If my tables below have any validity, the percentage would be lower. Otherwise I find in his speculations unfailing good judgment and an extraordinary penetration of the barrier of time; no one has done more to draw Will Langland into our range of vision. Donaldson argues that the inferiority of "C" to "B" poet has been exaggerated, and flatly disagrees with John Manly's description of a "petty, crotchety old man engaged in butchering someone else's work" and with Greta Hort's of an "intelligent and meddlesome scribe."[7] In the C version, Donaldson goes on to say, the poet often removes naïve expressions, makes sharp wording less biting, moralizes on what has been said in B, and (most important in relation to the present study) *generalizes* significantly.

III *Comparative Textual Analysis*

There are good reasons why further comparative analysis of the three versions should not be postponed. The most obvious reason —the lacuna in Langland criticism—is the result of the neglect of close reading of the three texts together, word by word. Individually, each has had all the illumination that a large company of British, American, German, French, and Oriental medievalists could give. As a unit, however, this poem-in-three-versions still stands in almost total darkness. The task of collateral reading will not be completed without the solid underpinning of the new editions, and an interpretation written today and based to any extent on statistics may very well require modification or partial or even total refutation when all the collations are available. The analysis which I offer below was made with full realization of the speculative risks involved; I have limited myself to patterns in Langland's growth and change, backed by such large frequency counts that even if a goodly portion of citations for one pattern are the work of scribes, not Langland, the remainder will still constitute impressive evidence of the validity of the pattern (e.g., frequency of *all* in C which suggests a more tolerant and catholic view of life in the older poet).

Another point in defense of going ahead with the kind of cross-reading I have made is the faultiness of the archetype manuscript from which all the other copies are descended. Lacking as we do autograph manuscripts of the three texts, we can never be certain of Langland's intention at each and every point; and years from now, when the poem is mined over and over again by scholars working within the security of sound editions, final judgments will still rest partly on recurring rather than on isolated features. One emendation might have been made by anybody; one hundred of the same thing must have been made by William Langland. Lengthy deletions and additions in B and C will always be taken on faith as Langland's; however, without autograph manuscripts or copies known to have had Langland's approval, there will be at that future date, as there are today, strong indications of scribal tinkering and scribal error.

One other reason for my decision to publish the results of my word-by-word comparison of the three texts is an impression, not to say a strong one, made by various collations of some of the manuscripts: Skeat's variant readings for all texts; George Kane's for A. In David C. Fowler's notes on A there are only samplings of the thousands of variants among the manuscripts of A; but these, plus his variants indicating genetic relationships of several manuscripts, lead me to hope (since my patterns are scarcely touched by his variant readings) that scribes will someday be shown to have had little to do with setting up the pattern-making changes from A to B to C. Also, R. W. Chambers' *Introduction to Huntington Library Manuscript 142* contains F. A. R. Carnegy's readings (M.A. thesis, University of London, 1923).

In all of these notes a scribe's dialectal and literary idiosyncrasies sometimes rise to the surface, but thus far I do not see in the notes certain peculiar features which I tentatively attribute to Langland's own revisions and which constitute the main portion of the present chapter. I fully realize that, at some future date when the study has been completed by many hands, my "findings" will be in need of modification. Meanwhile, by gleaning after the heavy mowers and by attending to minuscule items that broader studies have passed over, I hope to sharpen the focus on the poet. My coming at the poem through analysis of individual words may seem suspiciously Wittgensteinian, but linguistic philosophy is not intended.

With all that has been written about *Piers Plowman*—much of it a help toward the understanding of a very difficult work, some of it unfortunately a darkening of the poem's obscurities and mysteries—there has been all too little discussion of lexical features. Rosenthal, Manly, Oakden, and others analyzed the element of alliteration; word-play has been receiving increased attention, but much more study of it is needed;[8] and various dialectal features have been classified. A considerable amount of comment has been given to the naturalness of Langland's diction and to the easy colloquialism of a large part of the work, both of which are symptoms of Langland's intention to speak to all social classes. The editors of the poem—Skeat most notably—have contributed critical notes on individual words. Kane's very perceptive analyses of substitutions by scribes deal with errors of assorted kinds, with the probable circumstances in which they occurred, and with revisions for clarification, emphasis, amplification. Scribes also made substitutions and additions, he says, in order to smooth a rough transition, to embellish the alliteration, or to improve the meter.

The editions-to-come of B and C will supply additional notes on lemmas and will round out the collation of manuscripts. But, even when that peak has been conquered, the ultimate convenience will still not have been provided the critics of *Piers Plowman*—a form of footnote for each word giving all variant readings from all manuscripts of all three texts. Without this convenience, which is, to put it mildly, too much to ask for, the scholar who is seeking to determine whether it is Langland, or a scribe, who is most likely maker of a revision in B or C will of necessity handle all three volumes—the three editions—laboriously locating in each volume the problematical item. Someone engaged in a very special study, say a comparison of metaphor in B and C, will search to the last variant. The general reader, however, will accept from the specialist a summary of the results of his study; the general reader will never do the whole job for himself. Since one scribe or another is going to intrude between the reader and Langland, some uncertainty will inevitably creep in. When, in addition, the author of the special study takes his place between Langland and the general reader, inevitably introducing something of his own bias, a degree of subjectivity will result.

The above pleading and protestation is all by way of justifying the present excursion into an area that might more wisely be left untouched a while longer. For what they are worth, here are certain small impressions of the evolution of a poet. The emphasis is on the last of his three states, at which time the wisdom, humanity, and idiosyncrasies of the man are even more strongly suggested in the emendations than is a gain or loss in the quality of Langland's art. The patterns discussed below are, in my opinion, keys to certain aspects of Langland's character. These patterns began to appear after I had gone through two obviously required steps: first, simultaneous readings and rereadings of Skeat's parallel texts; second, word-by-word notation of variations.

Numerous as the variations are, they might seem to offer proof of multiple authorship.[9] The conditions are lacking, however, in which such proof would exist; and the patterns into which the variations fall are, in the end, a reinforcement of the argument for single authorship. If there were variations marking complete departures from vocabulary established in the earlier version, or if the variations indicated interests or modes of thought alien to those of the earlier version, or, to make-believe for a moment, if

the author of C had followed A much more closely than he had, then the question of authorship might have to be reopened. I do not mean to suggest that it is closed tight—but there is today almost total agreement on Langland's authorship of the three versions. The name "Will Langland" is now generally specified in the index as well as the text of books on *Piers Plowman,* and in the learned journals. The fact is that from any view, long or short, broad or narrow, Langland is easily perceived in the process of growth, of aging.

In diction and rhetorical devices the three versions are remarkably unified. Langland's fondness for puns, for example, which makes one common denominator, is still so pronounced in the C text that he seems to me occasionally to make a substitution for the sake of yet another pun which only a most careful reader of the line in both versions would notice.[10] This practice, if it truly is one, constitutes a very private little joke.

As for the dependence of C on B, in preference to dependence on A, the statistics are very interesting. By my count, throughout all twelve passus of the A version and the corresponding first ten passus of the B version, in minor changes involving *one word* or *something less than a line,* C follows B and rejects A in almost precisely twice as many instances as it follows A and rejects B: from the beginning through Passus VI, 275 times for B, 140 for A; from VII through X, 445 for B, 210 for A. In Passus X and XI, the two-to-one ratio is lost in favor of B. The originator of a poem who spends several years reworking it and increasing its length will normally regard the second version as superior to the first; and in a third and final attempt to perfect the poem, while he may remember substantial portions of it in its earliest form and keep by him a copy of that form for reference, he will be inclined to use it much less than he does the version that followed it.

If another man had written C, after Langland had written A, this second poet, as a matter of choice, not only would most probably have used B exclusively as his model but might well have had no copy of A in his possession. It is highly unlikely that both A and B would have been as deeply êmbedded in his memory as Langland proved they were in his when he wrote C. It is my guess that only to their author would it have seemed necessary to excerpt and blend in C both of the earlier versions.

In setting up the many tables of this study which, it is hoped,

reveal something of Langland's character, I have made use of added and deleted passages of one or more lines rather more often than one-word emendations. One reason for adopting this procedure is my belief that it will reveal more about the man Langland if, as I surmise, his subconscious is more actively at work in the wording of the longer alterations. When he lifts out a single word and sets another in its place, his thinking in making the word-choice deserves more likely to be considered as conscious and deliberate. If style is the man, the subconscious can be said to be the writer.

CHAPTER 3

Patterns

THE poet's tendency toward line-expansion in C has drawn much comment. Not only are hundreds of the lines longer than in A and B, but there is a somewhat higher incidence of lines with three or more alliterations. As a result of this general filling out of the structure of his poem, Langland adds to the effects of sonority, and this should go without saying. Not so easily proved, but perhaps worthy of speculation, is an interpretation which attempts to go beyond the structure of the poem and to catch a glimpse of the man himself. With the three versions of *Piers Plowman*, we have the rare circumstance of three ages in the poet's life—young, middle-aged, and old. His revisions in the second and third stages are possibly indicative of some of his own traits and attitudes, though here we must use caution and not be swayed too much by random impressions.[1]

In the lengthened lines, there is an impression of progressively increasing self-confidence as Langland takes broader strokes, adding emphasis and other effects; there is a feeling of relaxation as he grows more experienced, an impression of enlargement of spirit borne out, for instance, by the frequency of *all* in B and its even greater frequency in C. The word is, I think, an index to the catholicity of the aging poet's personal philosophy.

I Adverbs

One of the most conspicuous ways in which Langland embellished and expanded his last version line by line was the insertion of adverbs, of which the lexical and syntactic variety is so great that the approach must somehow be narrowed. Using frequency as the criterion, I have therefore chosen from a long list *wel, ful,* and *al,* and adverbs ending in *-liche.*

a   ADVERBS IN -LICHE

In a small way the suffix *-liche* is itself probably a part of the evolution toward a longer line: adverbs with *-ly* (or no suffix) are often replaced by an adverb ending in *-liche*. C has proportionately more of the *-liche* forms than does B, and the other adverbs (intensives) to be considered are found in C in significant numbers. It can therefore be conjectured that Langland in his old age had more savor for the extra syllable with its richness of sound and fullness of body. Some of his *-liche* adverbs in C also indicate greater interest in ideals (*leeliche* [loyally], *wisliche, parfitliche, sothliche*) and in the element of gentleness (*curteisliche, kyndeliche, softeliche, myldeliche, pacientliche*). By contrast, *dedliche, carefulliche* (mournfully), *caitifliche* (meanly), *grysliche* (grisly) and adverbs of their order appear in C only once. The emphatic *sikerliche* (certainly), and *witerliche*, its synonym, are used more often in C.

The poet also worked consciously with *-liche* in B in emendations of one line or more, but he deleted from A only three adverbs with this suffix in the first ten passus and added twelve not found in A (Prol., two; IV, two; V, three; VII, one; X, four)—too few to be called a strong trend and yet sufficient to be slightly symptomatic. In emendations of one line or more in the first twelve passus of C, which correspond to the first ten in B, there are fifty-eight additions of adverbs with *-liche;* only ten others are deleted, and four of these are bunched in Passus V. In emendations of less than one line there are thirty-four additions and seven deletions; occurrences in B are negligible. Apparently Langland was more readily impelled toward expansion when he was adding a whole line or lines; he would plainly have more room in which to introduce a polysyllabic adverb.

Beyond C XII, where the A version ends, and through the remaining eleven passus, the adverbial suffix *-liche* is found slightly more regularly than in the first twelve passus. Despite the fact that Langland was originating in B and merely revising in C, there are approximately twice as many additions in the later version. There are, moreover, disproportionately large numbers of additions in certain passus beyond XV—seventeen in XVII, for example, and fifteen in XX—possibly showing increasing fondness for the form. The average number of additions for all the passus in C is nearer ten. I have detected only three instances in this part of the poem in which the *-liche* form is found in B, the *-ly* form in C: they are *trewely,* C XXII, 177, and *trewliche,* B XIX, 172; *leelly,* C XXII, 181, and *leelich,* B XIX, 176; *cortesly* C XXIII, 243, and *curteislich,* B XX, 242.

To describe the change in the poet in terms of his use of adverbs, we might survey the great assortment of these adverbs which he inserted in C and then extract from them a few that illuminate the writer's process. We have already observed possible signs of an elevation of his ideals; it might also be said that the older Langland wrote more mildly (he deleted numerous oaths, as we shall see) but retained his force of conviction and intensified and emphasized with adverbs when he felt the moral or rhetorical need.

b ADVERBS IN WEL AND FUL

Wel, ful, and *al* are further examples of intensives, along with *sothliche, witerliche, sikerliche, soueraynliche, pureliche, riȝtfulliche, propreliche, fulliche, oneliche, heyȝliche, treweliche, gretliche. Wel* is most conspicuously used as a manner of doing or acting in Dowel. Where it is used conventionally, *wel* has the effect of intensifying, much as it does today in "well he knew"; but the usage had greater strength in Middle English. Its relative loss of force as an intensifier in Modern English is evidenced in its frequent modification by *very,* and in the narrowness of its usage as compared with the wide range of its adaptability in Middle English. We limit ourselves today to a few trite constructions (verbs of action like *swim, drive, dance* and verbs of performing like *sing, play, write*), at times implying with a certain intonation "well enough," which is not very intensive. We still use it to intensify past participles ("well disciplined") and the adjective *aware.* Its use as a hypercorrect adjective having nothing to do with health need not be discussed ("It will be well to consider . . .").

In *Piers Plowman* the word presents quite another appearance, or variety of appearances: before adjective complements ("God was wel the wrother" [C I, 117]); as modifier of *like* and *love* where today "very much" is used; of adverbs (*wel faste* [B Prol., 67]), (*wel fer* [far] [B XI, 34]).

It functions in Middle English, thus, with the meanings of the modern adverbs *very, quite, rather, much,* and *right* (*wel* [Kane

fete] sone [A XII, 47]). In *Piers Plowman* the intensive is the
dominant usage, though all the other denotations have generous
distribution. Langland made sparing use of the intensive in the A
version, and then in his B version—the most descriptive, dramatic,
and lyrical of the three—he increased the frequency of *wel*, as the
following tabulation gives evidence. The citations are from passages of one line or more added in the B and C versions; single-
word substitutions (e.g., *wel* for *ful*) are negligible in number
(one per passus) and are not given. These additions of *wel* in the
B version (Prol. through X, one or more lines) are: Prol.—152,
207; III—54; IV—31, 181; V—141, 179, 193, 264, 266, 426; VI—
47, 198, 204; VIII—52; IX—39, 92, 94; X—397, 431.

Langland's dependence on *wel* as an emphatic word is more
greatly increased in C (over B, Prol. through X) than it was in B
(over the twelve passus of A). B V, for example, has six additions
of *wel*, all of which are faithfully repeated in C. To these, four
more are added. Because both A and B went into the making of
the first twelve passus of C and because in some places Langland
deleted *wel* from both A and B and also added *wel* in others, thus
complicating the emendations considerably, I have tabulated all
additions of *wel* in C. All passus are included. Additions of *wel* in
the C version (I—XII, one or more lines) are: I—100, 103, 117;
II—132; III—47; IV—141; V—21, 52, 53, 154, 183; VI—8, 182;
VII— 48 (2), 108, 419; VIII—300; X—128, 147, 244; XI—187 (2),
200, 202, 239, 260; XII—225.

Langland's dependence on *wel* as an emphatic word is, thus,
somewhat increased in C (over B) in the first part of the poem:
twenty-eight additions against twenty. Two considerations add to
the significance of these totals. First, although there are a few
deletions of *wel* from B in the C revision, these are offset by the
short emendations adding *wel* in C; and the fact is that C assimi-
lates from A and B almost as many instances of *wel* as it contrib-
utes, so that the total of twenty-eight additions in C may be considered as being actually almost doubled. Second, both *wel* and
ful should be looked at as particles merely playing supporting
roles to the third particle *al*, which looms so large in all parts of
the poem. *Wel* and *ful* belong to what I take to be an important
aspect of Langland's revision.

After B X, all balance in the addition of *wel* is lost. I find sev-
enty-two additions in B and only four in C in the second half of

the poem (B X—XX, C XIII—XXIII), which we can assume
to have been written later than the first half. Some of these passus
in C may have been written not months but years later when
Langland was getting on—nearer old than middle age. Numbers
of additions of *wel* as adverb in the individual passus are: B XI,
ten; XII, six; XIII, ten; XIV, nine; XV, nine; XVI, four; XVII, six;
XVIII, three; XIX, seven; XX, eight. The average number per
passus is 7.2, and eight of the passus are so consistent that a claim
of deliberate design seems almost justified.

In the C version there is also consistency, but of a negative
kind. I have noticed only four additions of *wel* as adverb in the
last ten passus, one each in XIV, XVII, XIX, and XXIII. As has
been already observed, it may have been the older poet who
made the additions in B XI—XX. In any case, he would find
fewer opportunities for this kind of emendation in the last revision.

The adverb *ful* is, in comparison with *wel*, restricted in function
and in frequency. Its function is the modification of adjectives and
adverbs as a mild intensive, and the function of *ful* in *Piers Plowman* can thus be said to be the complementing of *wel*, which usually modifies verbs. *Ful* makes relatively rare appearances; and,
since in C it is deleted almost as many times as it is added, *ful*
loses most of the significance it might have had in Langland's patterning. Only in the last passus of B does it suddenly burst into
prominence, appearing seven times. Otherwise, it is added, if at
all, from one to three times in B and less than an average of one
time per passus in C.

C THE USE OF AL

Al, which I have saved to the last of the adverbs, is much more
active as an adjective and as a noun than as an adverb; consequently, it is discussed as all three parts of speech.

The phenomenal ubiquity of *al* makes this word a surer indication than any of the words already treated that Langland worked
to increase the force of his message and that his attitude toward
society and all the types of its members became progressively
more tolerant and comprehensive. By the time of the writing of
the C version, he is thinking usually of large numbers and totali-
ties,[2] seldom of *some* men, very often of *alle manere* men. In part,
this wide-flung embrace is the characteristic and perfectly noble

posture of a true Christian; and, this being so, Langland has perhaps succeeded in ending as an even better Christian than he began. In part, he is spreading his opened hands in an old man's shrug of resignation. "In this late day," he seems to be saying, "let us speak in generalities." They are what count when time is short, not particular little cases and strange individuals. To catch the big issues and the changeless generalities, he uses a strong net with a wide mesh and is content to let the anomalies slip through. His own growth in capacity for love parallels in a small way the arrival at Dobest, represented by the emergence of Piers-Christ as the Savior of all men.

Undoubtedly, a man of Langland's satiric gifts and disposition must have had in his younger years a certain astringency as a conversationalist; his facility with biting words, nourished by his idealist's impatience with the world, would have made him feared by the very friends whom he most fascinated. But perhaps his asperities lessened as he grew older—not the usual course in a man's pattern of behavior, to be sure. After a lifetime of meditation on salvation and a prolonged effort to help his brothers to align their spiritual values more accurately, perhaps his preoccupation with grace, good works, and eternity became dominant. These interests forced mundane concerns into a back place, one not to be disregarded (C preserves the substance of B and has besides a slightly stronger vein of earthiness) but one which no longer possessed the all-shadowing importance that sharpens the reactions of worldly men. Admittedly, sexagenarian mellowing cannot be deduced from the proliferation of *al* as adjective, noun, and adverb; I only offer the idea as a possibility. In following pages a few additional clues (Langland's use of oaths, for example) will be adduced.

Lest it appear that the interpretation of *al* as a pattern of tolerance and benevolence jars with what has already been said about the other intensives (for *al* sometimes intensifies), I should make the point that *wel, ful,* and the adverbs in -*liche* do not possess in most of their usages a rhetorical capacity for violence or even much force. The main reason why this is so is, I believe, their very frequency, which, on the one hand, tells us much about Langland's sincerity and his eagerness to be morally influential but also, on the other hand, has a leveling and blunting effect. More important than this qualification is the fact that Langland's intensives do subtly underscore the lesson being taught; and, appearing primarily in passages that are even in tone and restrained in diction, they have little to do with fits of passion and emotional outbursts. These intensives, then, reinforce the poet's argument; and they are thus to be perceived as raising in a limited way the spiritual level of the poem. (We shall see that the word *heuene* [heaven] works to the same purpose.)

Since, as a general rule, *al* is intensive only in its function as an adverb, it may for the sake of continuity in the topic of intensification be considered first as an adverb, despite its relative rarity. It should be borne in mind that, along with its intensive function, the adverb *al*, like the adjective and noun, in most of its applications in *Piers Plowman* carries a denotation of inclusiveness and therefore adds its bit to the grand impression made by Langland's love of the form *al*.

The pattern begins in B; the adverb figures very modestly, but an indication of Langland's degree of dependence on it in B facilitates appreciation of the increase in C. Additions to A are the most significant in this connection.

Prol.—X (*One or more lines*):

Additions of *al* as adverb in B (over A): B II—39, 124; V—197, 295, 392; IX—152.

Deletions in B of *al* as adverb (from A): A II—41; VI—5; VII —186; VIII—155.

I—XII (*Short emendations*):

Additions of *al* as adverb in C (over B): C I—178; II—75; VI—163.

Deletions in C of *al* as adverb (from B): C III—177; V—147.

C I—XII (*One or more lines*):

Additions of *al* as adverb in C (over B): C IV—203; V—183; VII—23; XII—62.

Deletions in C of *al* as adverb (from B): B IX—152; X—290; XI—169.

B XI—XX, C XIII—XXIII:

Additions of *al* as adverb in B: B XI—50, 110, 348, 390; XII— 255; XIII—141; XIV—11; XV—40, 138, 352, 548; XVI—18, 80; XVIII—3, 106, 246, 306; XIX—6, 163; XX—112.

Additions of *al* as adverb in C (over B): C XIV—127; XVII— 266; XIX—39; XXI—63, 292; XXII—365.

The relative sparsity of the adverb *al* ads little to a survey of

Langland's intensive adverbs, but it does, in view of the very numerous appearances of *al* as adjective and noun, cited below,
focus almost to a single beam the effect of the form *al*—it is not as
an intensive adverb but as an inclusive adjective and noun that
Langland uses *al* both in B and in C nine-tenths of the time. If *al*
is taken as a key to his purpose and if the other adverbs are kept
in mind, it can be said that he was concerned about emphasis and
that, with much restraint of diction, he dispersed a few intensive
forms but that inclusiveness was his *constant* concern.

   B Prol.—X: sixty-four additions in B of *al* as adjective (over A)
(one or more lines); thirteen deletions in B of *al* as adjective
(from A) (one or more lines); forty-two additions in C of *al* as
adjective (over B) (short emendations); seventy-seven additions
in C of *al* as adjective (over B) (one or more lines); eighteen
deletions in C of *al* as adjective (from B) (short emendations);
thirty-seven deletions in C of *al* as adjective (from B) (one or
more lines).

   B XI—XX, C XIII—XXIII: 247 additions of *al* as adjective in
B; one hundred additions in C of *al* as adjective (over B); seventy-
eight additions of *al* as noun in B; nineteen additions of *al* as noun
in C (over B). (See Appendix for line numbers.)

   The significant totals from the tabulations are as follows. From
the beginning through the end of A in passages of one or more
lines which are not found in A, there are 224 additions of *al*. B and
C are almost even here, with the ratios six to four (adverb), sixty-
four to seventy-seven (adjective), twenty-six to twenty (noun).
Considering that the additions in C are overlaid on the older
stratum of B, we are safe in concluding that the poet was even
more eager in his last revision than at the middle stage to speak in
universals, seeing all men as brothers with a common nature, making blanket indictments of evil, and exhibiting the human race
now in the light of its goodness and again in the shadow of sin.

   Working with fewer opportunities, he yet managed to repeat
his earlier performance in B when he was already mounting toward a broadly tolerant view (if tolerant is taken to mean recep-
tive, not permissive). He had, to be sure, shown his catholic disposition in the first passus of the A version, the first page in fact,
when he peopled the field in the vision with a cross section of
humanity. Often the wording of A survives into B, and *al* is not
added until the C version is reached; for example:

> "And alle that wrong worchen wende thei schulen
> After heore deth-day and dwellen with that schrewe."
> (A I, 117–18)

This statement is unchanged in B, and *alle* remains in C, though
wrong is replaced by *wikkede* (another word frequently adopted
in C to add emphasis, as we shall see). Changes in the next lines
are more revealing:

> "Ac heo that worchen that word that holi writ techeth
> And endeth as Ich er seide in profitable werkes,
> Mouwen be siker [certain] that heore soules schullen to heuene."
> (A I, 119–20)

In B *that word* is replaced by *wel. Heo* (A) and *tho* (B) are
replaced by *Alle* in C. Langland seems to have resisted immediate
repetition of *al* in A and B, but with his increased preference for
al in C the repetition is a natural reflex.

In this portion of the poem, which is called the "Visio" (the
entire A version and corresponding passus in B and C), the adjective *al* is dominant over adverb and noun. Syntax thus lends another clue to Langland's attitude, since *al* as adjective universal-
izes in a way that is beyond the power of the intensive adverb *al;*
and *al* the noun, actually a demonstrative pronoun deriving from
the adjective, implicitly carries with it the meaning of some other,
more specific noun. In short, the demonstrative noun has an adjec-
tival function.

In the second half of the poem, the "Vita" (B X—XX, C XIII—
XXIII), of which B is the original version, it is to be expected that
innovations in B will be proportionately more numerous, since
there is no A version to preclude any of them. The B text therefore
goes beyond C in the number of additions of *al;* in C, however,
the poet is still building on B, as he did in the Visio. The much-
modified ratios are: twenty-one / six (adverb), two hundred forty-
seven / one hundred (adjective), seventy-eight / nineteen (noun).

Altogether, in both B and C, *al* appears in emendations of all
lengths about 672 times.

Although the distribution of the form is fairly even overall, a
few discrepancies of a positive type are worth noting. *Al* occurs as
a single part of speech in strings: two per line; and one per line for

two or more lines: adjective, C IV—374 (2); VII—437 (2); B
XV—164 (2), 553 (2); XVII—129 (2), 246 (2); XVIII—223 (2),
425 (2); C IV—388–89; VIII—258–59; XIX—238–39, XX—103–
104; B V—180–81, 289–90; X—279–80; XIII—123–24; XIV—298–
299; XVIII—106–7, 351–52, 394–95, 402–3; XX—59–60; B V—
485–6–7; XVIII—253–54–55; XIX—425 (2)–6 [also 423]. Alter-
nating lines are also interesting: B Prol.—175, 177, 179, 181, 183
[also 186–87]; XIII—167, 169, 171, 173.

For the simple reason that Langland scarcely jarred a word out
of place in transferring B XIX to C XXII and B XX to C XXIII,
there is a decrease in the number of additions of *al* when C XXII
is reached. Dramatic excitement is not lacking in these passus,
particularly in the passages in which the Dreamer narrates the
coming of Antichrist; but the tenor of the passus is one of ending
and departure. A kind of peace has been reached, Conscience
goes on with resignation rather than with bounding hope to
search for Piers, and Langland himself seems to have found a degree of detachment from his earlier bitter concern. At the conclu-
sion of the B text, he had reviewed with a more paternal eye the
fair field, including the friars. Years later, having spent a whole
lifetime peering into men's hearts and writing and preaching reform, he could bend his tall frame more protectively over his poor
friend Everyman; and with sympathy and good humor he let him
do his stumbling best to get to heaven. His own strong lesson on
patience seems to have had as much effect on himself as on any of
his audience.

To the old poet thus conditioned—neither despairing of man's
destiny nor idealizing his prospects but finding the whole human
comedy a little less unbearable against a background of some sixty
years of rigorous living—the ending that he had made to *Piers
Plowman* when he first wrote the Vita, in B, must have fitted well
with his attitude and objective as he came to the ending of C.
Both in this last passus and in the opening two passus Langland
made comparatively few changes, and so it may be said that his
world-view first and last is essentially unchanged, but that within
the poem his personal reactions to the beauties and horrors and
vexations of life are not unvarying. He reacts more truly as a poet
when he is younger, he reacts differently to the various characters
and to different clerical types, he changes his stylistic approaches.

It is fascinating to watch the rise and fall of the gauge of emotionalism.

In the last two passus, as we have seen, B is transferred almost intact to C; *al* is scarcely touched. There are, however, fairly normal uses of *al* in XIX and XX. It is used as adverb twice in XIX, once in XX; as adjective, forty-three times in XIX, twenty-six in XX; as noun, fourteen times in XIX, three in XX. The totals are fifty-nine against thirty. We would anticipate a gradual tempering of Langland's feelings in the concluding passus, and the relative frequencies of *al* reflect it.

Over a span of seventy thousand words he has sought and tried to summon and save all men; he has strained to build a frame around all of creation. How human he is now to let up, feeling no doubt that, if the multitude are to hear his voice, they have already heard it in the many passus that precede the last one.

Deletions of *al* merit a few words of discussion before the subject is closed, even though these excisions merely add support to the observations already made and bring into light very little that is otherwise unsaid. The most important point to be made is that deletions of *al* in a given set never outnumber additions and are for the most part fractional; Langland's design is thus placed in bolder relief. In the Visio, which is revised by B and in turn by C, the percentage of deletions is many times greater than that in the Vita; in fact, deletions of *al* are so scarce in the Vita that I have not recorded them. But the first half of the poem has been drastically overhauled twice by Langland, and for many reasons other than pinpoint placement of the form *al*. To look to deletions for patterns of momentous significance would, therefore, be a misguided effort; *al* is frequently jettisoned along with other more important cargo because it happens to be attached to what Langland has decided to drop from A and B.

However, *additions* of *al* incorporated in longer passages are quite possibly to be regarded along with individual insertions of the word as signs of Langland's broadening humanity. Far from being a mere incidental excrescence on the interpolated passages, *al* is frequently the key word around which Langland has built an idea; one example is the passage quoted on page 43 which deals with the happy fate of right-doers, *all* of whom are saved in C, and presumably in A and B, too, with the difference that the less inclusive pronouns *heo* and *tho* are used, respectively. Langland meant these pronouns to refer to everyone who "worked well," but it was not until he was writing the C version that it occurred to him (or he finally decided) to use the repetitious but explicitly inclusive word *al*.

Other examples abound, especially when people are involved. Whether he speaks of kings, merchants, bishops, sinners, or simply all men, the word *al* is indispensable by the time Langland is writing the C version. On a still wider plane is the demonstrative pronoun *al*, already discussed, which is capable of representing all members of any type or class of people. In my observation it is used not so voluminously as is the adjective.

In an effort to widen his scope Langland sometimes stops short of the ultimate form *al*. In doing so, the device to which he resorts most frequently is grammatical number, going from singular to plural, adding numerals where none had been, simply adding to or multiplying a number in B to make a larger one in C, and inserting the word *many*. As with *al*, the poet is in the latest stage (the C version) when he most freely introduces the larger numbers. Quantitatively the tabulations below are not very impressive, but as a supplement to the *al* pattern they gain significance; they are an offshoot of the grand pattern of inclusiveness.

II *Number*

Additions of a numeral in C: C II—84; IV—41; V—61; X—315; XVI—81; XVII—9; XXI—62.

Deletions of a numeral from B: B II—54; V—377; XIII—427.

Plurals made in C on singulars in B: C VI—159 (2); VII—98, 219; IX—229; XII—7, 39, 163, 277, 297; XV—45, 53; XVI—11; XVII—19, 39, 47, 104, 134, 150, 223, 340; XVIII—47, 25; XX—64; XXI—37, 101, 103, 424.

Singulars made in C on plurals in B: VIII—47, 49; XII—5; XIII —21, 77; XV—79; XVI—275; XVII—210, 214, 245, 349; XVIII— 47, 181; XXI—365, 433; XXII—60, 389, 437; XXIII—128.

Higher number in C: VIII—17, 29; X—343; XV—3; XXI—311.

Higher number in B: IV—41; VIII—188; XVI—69, 272; XX— 24; XXIII—218.

Additions of *many* in C: III—57; IV—13; VII—73, 96, 428; XI —87; XII—50, 163; XV—190.

Deletions of *many* from B: C V—67 (C *largelich*); VI—166; VIII—49; X—41 (C *somme*).

III *Heuene*

Langland's empathy with everything that God ever made—an affinity that is strongest in C—is mirrored peculiarly in his treatment of the word *heuene* in the C text. For an old man on the verge of knocking at heaven's gate, the temptation to dwell on the idea of heaven can be irresistible. It was not so for Langland, if he is judged according to the frequency of specific references to heaven in the C text. Like the Chaucer who wrote the fabliaux, the old man Langland seemingly could not hold the world close enough; could only look with compassion and amusement, tempered with wisdom, on the antics of his fellows; and, with an eternity of heaven possibly stretching before him, clutched the world he knew, reluctant to give it up so soon. Passus XII, XIV, and XVIII in B have to do with salvation; Passus XV is about charity and a cleric's responsibilities; and all four have concentrations of the word *heuene*. Passus XIII, a down-to-earth description of a dinner party and the sin soiled appearance of Haukyn, significantly contains no additions of *heuene*.

Without ever letting up in his preoccupation with the means of salvation and his altruist's zeal as a guide to it, Langland makes an obvious shift in the direction of his thought on the subject. During his closing years he becomes less attentive to the end, heaven itself; but he maintains all of his interest in the means to it. There is no question of indifferentism or loss of faith; the old poet's sensibilities, which are hyperacute because Langland is a poet and which are still keenly awake in the evening of his life, commit him to the fascinations of the natural and social world. He may have lost some of his poet's fire and rage, but he is vitally aware.

His deliberate expunging in C of the word *heuene* and of passages containing the word is on a scale sufficiently large that some slight alteration of his attitude can be inferred. Moreover, the count of forty deletions of heaven in C, in comparison with only twenty-nine additions, is contrary to Langland's usual practice of adding much and removing little. The number of additions in B, on the other hand, suggests that heaven both as a habitation and a name was much in his thoughts at the middle stage.

B Prol.—X

Additions of *heuene* in B: Prol.—106, 127, 128, 209; I—118, 121, 146, 149, 151, 157, 203; II—33; IV—179; V—56, 278; VI—47; VII —53; IX—45, 99, 101, 117, 126; X—300.

C I—XII

Additions of *heuene* in C: I—133; II—104, 108, 133; III—33, 38, 132; IV—98, 459; VI—59, 187; VII—308, 318, 331; VIII—136, 249; X—126; XII—200.

Deletions of *heuene* from B (Prol.—X): B Prol.—128, 209; I— 118, 121, 130; II—33; III—50; V—516; VI—223; IX—46, 99, 101, 117, 126; X—334, 343, 352.

B XI—XX

Additions of *heuene* in B: XI—81, 179; XII—38, 68, 128, 141, 211, 212, 281; XIV—65, 128, 141, 151, 154, 165, 209, 211, 260; XV—51, 170, 345, 399, 450, 472, 539; XVI—118, 208, 213, 222; XVII—144, 161, 163, 200, 243; XVIII—222, 237, 277, 309, 318, 354, 395; XIX—77, 186; XX—193, 268, 274.

C XIII—XXIII

Additions of *heuene* in C: XVII—27, 170, 309; XVIII—149, 247; XIX—72, 88, 89, 91, 98; XXI—55.

Deletions of *heuene* from B (XI—XX): B XI—81, 179; XII—38, 68, 128; XIV—30, 128, 151, 154, 165; XV—170, 450, 472; XVI— 118, 208, 213, 222; XVII—161, 163; XVIII—277, 309, 354.

Heuene is deleted from B a total of forty times as Langland makes his last revision. He adds it in the C version a total of twenty-nine times. For an entirely different attitude toward the word, we compare the sum of additions in the B version—sixty-nine. I have not detected any losses of *heuene* in the transition from the A to the B versions, but there are seventeen deletions from B in the portion of C which has corresponding passus in the A version. Here I should guess the poet's practice to have been an unconscious one altogether; he would never have set out to prove that he was losing interest in the heavenly kingdom. But what he does do, it seems to me, is to tap the balance again in favor of the precious and fading here and now.

IV *Earthy Expressions*

As Langland abandons the word *heuene* at certain points in his text and indulges himself in a mild manner at this world's table, he helps himself to a number of earthy expressions which age's capacity for tolerance has rendered unobjectionable, or at least not unacceptable in comparison with the more straitened view of his middle years. These expressions are no doubt related to the intensive forms for which he also has shown a predilection in the C text: both strengthen the voice of the pulpit orator in his last appeal. The inference is inescapable that the worst people and the vilest matter seem a mite less evil to the church's old warrior now that time is growing short. In this respect he also shows himself to be like the Chaucer of the fabliaux.

Unlike the other specimens in the patterns of this study, the vulgarisms, both scatological and sexual, are difficult to isolate and classify; and at a distance of centuries we cannot hope even to approach the complete list known to Langland. What shall "earthy" designate? The word *dung* and all its synonyms are of the earth, disgustingly earthy to the hygienic society of our time. But to Langland and contemporaries the word was a commonplace of every day; and, though he would have made a broad distinction between *drit*, or *donge*, and *wolkene* (sky), he would be amused by the delicate shudders of modern reaction. For the sake of simplification, however, it can be assumed that Langland was consciously showing a very human side when he chose certain expressions.

Omitted from my list—there being no other choice—are all the doubtful words which by a semantic stretching might be called "earthy," today: *dronke, nyuylynge, slimy, lycame* [body].[3] Since the list cannot be exhaustive, I have chosen a representative group of single words and longer quotations. Additions of both types are rare when Langland is revising A, but they are numerous in the revisions in B.[4]

In B, *cokewolde* (B V–159), *ers* (B V–175; X–309), *harlotrie* (B IV–115; V–413; X–30) and *hore* (IV–166) are added—as are entire lines whose context coarsens the connotations of words which are normally quite neutral: Wrath, speaking of nuns he has known, says that he has spread the slander

". . . that dame Iohanne was a bastard,
And dame Clarice a kniȝtes douȝter ac a kokewolde [cuckold]
   was hire syre,
And dame Peronelle a prestes file priouresse worth she neuere,
For she had childe in chirityme al owre chapitere it wiste."
                                                (V, 158–61)

A little later he explains how he is "baleised [beaten] on the bare
ers and no breche bitwene"; and he says "I have a fluxe of a foule
mouthe wel fyve dayes after" (l. 175). In the same passus Sloth
tells how he will stay in bed "but if my taille-ende it made" (l.
395) and "ligge abedde in lenten an my lemman in myn armes"
(l. 417). With an added line, Glutton is made even more disgusting in B than in A. It is "guttis gunne to gothely [grumble] as two
gredy sowes." (l. 347); Holy Scripture condemns those who "Spit-
ten and spewen and speke foule wordes" (B X—40).

In the comparison between A and B, deletions offset what little
contrast is created by the few additions in B. The word *harlotrie*,
added in B V–413, had been deleted in A IV–106, though *harlotes*
was preserved two lines before. From A II–54–55 had been deleted the stipulation that Falseness should find Meed "boxum
[obedient] . . . in bedde"; from A V—70 (Envy speaking)

"Venim or vernisch or vinegre, I trouwe,
Walleth [wells] in my wombe or waxeth, ich wene.
I ne mihte mony day don as a mon ouhte,
Such wynt [wind] in my wombe waxeth, er I dyne."

Excised from A VII—169, where Piers has just smitten Hunger in
the lips with a "bean-bat," is "And he bledde in-to the bodiward a
bolleful of gruwel."

In the C text the earthy additions are more abundant in spite of
the fact that Langland assumed his familiar handicap in the making of additions to a text that was itself a revision containing additions of the same type. Lechery, for example, is given much fuller
treatment in C (VII). In order to keep the comparison of B and C
on an even basis, quotations will be limited to the first twelve
passus. As with B, single words will be listed first, followed by
sentences: *brake* (vomited) (VII, 431), *harlot* (VII, 369), *harlotrie* (IV, 302), (VIII, 76), *hore* (IV, 302), (VII, 149, 306), (VIII,

76), *queyne* (low woman) (IX, 46), *rybaudes* [ribalds] (VII, 435), *shiteth* (X, 264), *wantowen* (IV, 143).

The most representative *lines* are as follows:

"Til aither cleped othere 'hore' and of with the clothes,"
(VII, 149)

"Of puterie [lechery] and of paramours and proueden thorw speches,
Handlynge and halsynge [embracing] and al-so thorw cussynge
Excitynge oure aither other til oure olde synne;
Sotilede [invented] songes and sende out olde baudes
For to wynne to my wil wommen with gyle;
By Sorcerye som tyme and som tyme by maistrye.
Ich lay by the louelokeste [loveliest] and loued hem neuere after."
(VII, 186–92)

"For an hore of hure ers-wynnynge . . ." (VII, 306)
"And as an hounde that et gras so gan ich to brake," (VII, 431)
". . . the wolf shiteth woolle:" (X, 264)
". . . lofsom [lovable] a bedde . . . vnlofsom a bedde,"
(XI, 259, 262)

Deletions from B in these passus are very light; of single words, only one has come to my notice—*ers* (B X, 123)—but the whole "earthy" line, and it definitely is one, should be quoted: "I wolde his eye were in his ers and his fynger after." In C IV, 466, a most peculiar substitution suggests that Langland regarded *sprede donge* as not quite fit for all contexts. B III, 307–8, enumerating some of the activities possible for a man, reads, "Eche man to pleyye with a plow pykoys or spade, / Spynne, or sprede donge or spille hymself with sleuthe." But line 308 is rewritten in C IV, 466: "Spynnen, and spek of god and spille no tyme": Langland may have changed the line because he felt that working with a spade was much the same as working with a rake or any large implement in spreading dung; and, his love for redundancy notwithstanding, he might regard repetition within such a list as illogical. Or he may have feared that his audience would read coarse humor, a reflection on the peaceful man who beats his sword into a plowshare. The threat to the armed man's salvation is specified in the passage immediately preceding:

> For alle that bereth baselardes [daggers] bryght swerde, other launce,

Axe, other acchett other eny kynne wepne,
Shal be demed to the deth bote yf he do hit smythie
In-to sykel other into sithe to shar other to culter;

(461–64)

V   *Oaths*

Langland's increasing interest in adverbs of the intensive type
might have led us to expect that oaths, which are freely used in
Middle English narrative and dialogue, would keep pace with the
adverbs in frequency. In a perfectly understandable paradox of
behavior, having intermittently eschewed the word *heuene* at the
same time that he was drawn to the use of a great number of
earthy expressions, Langland asserts his spirituality—in a sense
acknowledges an access of the fear of God—by distinctly curtail-
ing profane utterance in the C version. His is the God / man relationship on the highest plane; the intimacy of his new understanding instills in Langland greater respect for the dignity of God, and
leaves him disinclined to play lightly on the divine names or on
soul, faith, St. Paul, Mary, holy orders, the rood, (God's) life—
anything that has to do directly with the deity. This is not to say,
however, that the evidence points toward belated awareness of
the second Commandment. Early in the A version, in a kind of
pilgrim's progress to Truth with Piers giving directions, Piers as-
signs to one place the name "Swere-not-but-thou-haue-neode- /
And-nomeliche-in-idel-the-nome-of-god-almihti" (A VI, 60–61).

As with the other patterns, comparison will be made between B
and C on the basis of additions and deletions. Mild oaths of a non-
religious nature, which figure in this comparison on a small scale
(such as *maugre my chekes, by this day*), are not included. Line
numbers are dispensed with; a number of the oaths are used more
than once, yet the totals under B and under C are too small,
alongside those of such patterns as *-liche* and *al*, to be of statistical
value.

Distinct impressions are, nevertheless, received. In B, the additions of oaths outnumber the deletions by approximately seven to
one; in C, the deletions outnumber the additions by approximately twenty-five per cent. Because of the special rhetorical nature of oaths and their resultant sparsity, it was necessary to take
samples from all passus in order to get usable representations.

Additions in B are: bi Cryst (4), so god me help (3), bi god

(3), haue god my treuthe (2), wot god (2), bi my soule hele (2), bi Marie (2), bi the rode (2), god leue neure, goddes soule, lorde it the for-ȝelde, by my feith, bi his lyue, as Cryste wolde, as Cryst bereth witnesse, haue god my soule, by oure lorde, the fende haue his soule, goddes forbode elles. (Besides these, Langland makes original use of *swore* in B three times—once in V, twice in XIII.)

Deletions in B are: so me god helpe (2), bi crist, god wot the sothe (*othes* is deleted twice).

Additions in C: by Cryst (4), Seint Marye my lady (2), Lord, haue God my treuthe, Iesus wot the sothe, by good faith, as god wole, by the ordre that I bere, deere God, by my soule, for Cristes loue of heuene, Lord leyue.

Deletions in C: bi Crist (3), by Seynt Poule (2), god gyf the sorwe, bi god that me made, so me god helpe, bi god, god wote, god leue neure, haue god my treuthe, by seynt Marie my lady, bi the rode of Chestre, lorde it the for-ȝelde, for mercies sake, by my feith (besides these, Langland deletes *I swere, othes,* and *cursed*).

Predictably the two forms that figure most frequently are God and Cryst. In C, God is added three times but deleted seven; in B, added fourteen times and deleted only once. Cryst is added five times in C, deleted three; it is added six times in B, deleted only once.

All additions and deletions considered, it may therefore be said that the reader of the three versions could, without attempting to make a count, detect the higher content of oaths, both pious and profane, in the B version.

VI *Wikkede*

If his use of the word *wikkede* is an indication, Langland seems to have felt a little less condemnatory toward wicked folk when he wrote the C version. A strong case cannot be made that this adjective affords proof of a mellowing process in the aging satirist —citations are too few; A and B are too close in totals; and the slightly larger total of additions in B is undoubtedly due to the complete originality of the last ten passus in B. Also, as with other patterns already discussed, the near parity of C is impressive because of the existence of the preceding texts whose additions of the form in question had narrowed the possibilities for further additions. The deletions in C, however, will be seen to have some significance.

The following line references are to *wikkede* (and *wikke*), *wikkedliche,* and *wikkedness.* Additions of *wikkede* and derivatives in B are: B I—122; IV—62; V—152, 162, 180, 187, 229, 267, 290, 435; X—24; XIII—321; XV—125, 126, 164, 349; XVI—27, 34, 146, 157; XVII—285, 312, 317, 328; XVIII—383, 413; XIX—193, 281, 350, 375, 437; XX—267, 300, 368. The deletion of wikkede (no derivatives) in B is A X—65.

Additions of *wikkede* and derivatives in C: C II—130; IV—206; VII—334; VIII—118; IX—234; XI—236; XII—272, 273; XV—25, 135, 165, 167; XVII—177, 241; XX—102, 246; XXI—436. Deletions of *wikkede* and derivatives in C: B I—122; V—152, 162, 187, 229, 290; VI—1; VIII—96; IX—205; X—24, 427; XIII—321; XV—164; XVI—146, 157.

The form is added thirty-three times in B and seventeen times in C. It is deleted twice in B; fifteen times in C. Ten of these deletions take place within the first ten passus of B. Only ten of the additions in B, however, are found in the first ten passus. These figures suggest conscious discrimination against the form in the C version.

VII *Peple*

Langland's concern with people need not be re-emphasized. Nor can it be said that his social conscience or his desire to help all men toward salvation became more acute as he grew older. These attitudes, like his very flesh and bone, were constituent in the man. But there does seem, particularly in B, to be a sharpening of focus, the result of years of unflagging service in the cause of humanity; and it seems that the constant application of his energies and thoughts to the human problem shaped his style after a time and created the many patterns now being discussed. One such pattern, though not so boldly defined as the intensives, including oaths, is seen in the word *peple,* as common a word as any in the language. It can, however, be replaced by a number of equally common synonyms, and in many lines of the A version where *peple* would have been appropriate, *folk, men,* and pronouns, both personal and indefinite, are found. For the reader who does not go beyond the A version, *peple* will not register as a word of significant recurrence.

Its role changes in the B version; Langland continues to use it conservatively throughout the ten passus based on A, adding it a few times but deleting it almost as many. Once free of A, however, it is as though he discovers the full value of the unpretentious little noun and with virtually no deletions adds *peple* in over fifty lines.

In C he continues the additions, but deletions fall into normal proportions, indicating that his concentration on man has been relieved to some extent, possibly by the knowledge that he, William Langland, will soon stand alone to be judged. These deletions are complete; Langland does not merely reinsert the synonymous *folk, men,* and pronouns. Now, in his loyalty to the form *peple* it appears to me that he is acting from the same motivation that brought about such heavy use of *al.*

I find only six additions of *peple* in "short" revisions in the first ten passus of the C text. Additions in revisions of one or more lines average fewer than 0.5 per passus, I—XXIII. The great preponderance of additions of *peple* in B, however, occurs in revisions of one or more lines: II—57; III—299; V—23, 106, 146; VI—165; VII—95, 146; VIII—109; X—200; XI—108, 153, 169, 176, 178, 381; XII—74, 112, 159; XIII—176, 236, 250, 259, 278, 283, 313; XIV—72, 174, 194, 289; XV—70, 77, 88, 98, 197, 320, 382, 395, 530, 562, 581; XVI—251; XVII—35, 335; XVIII—36, 80, 418; XIX—7, 128, 337, 358, 418, 426, 452; XX—85, 97, 108, 124, 126, 278.

Deletions of *peple* in B revision (one or more lines): A Prol.— 93; II—40, 152; V—12; VIII—49; XI—195, 300; XII—102.

Additions of *peple* in C (all emendations): II—195; III—198; IV—81, 376, 386, 389; VI—116, 194; IX—190, 205; X—20, 34, 43; XII—16, 21, 268, 293, 294; XIII—120, 164; XVI—10, 70, 195, 232; XVII—94, 243; XVIII—34, 60, 69, 84, 94, 177, 180; XIX—86.

Deletions of *peple* in C revision (all emendations): B V—23, 105, 106, 146; VI—165; VII—10, 30, 95; VIII—109; X—200, 212; XI—153, 169, 178, 381; XII—74, 112, 159; XIII—176, 250; XIV— 72, 174, 194; XV—70, 88, 98, 197, 320, 321, 530, 581; XVI—251; XVII—35, 335; XVIII—6; XX—126. Of the eleven deletions from the first ten passus of the B text, the surprising total of six are deletions of passages which had been inserted in the B text as additions to A.

VIII   *Pore, Riche, and Syluer*

Writers and other types of artists of the first magnitude find an audience after little or much struggle, but they find it. That audience in the general course of events rewards the writer with little or much, but it does so reward him. In the case of Will Langland, whose writings barely skirt anonymity, things developed otherwise; we have no way of comparing the treatment accorded him by patrons and public with that of other medieval authors now anonymous, but we can speculate with some confidence that he received next to nothing in comparison with Chaucer; also with a large number of lesser lights—Lydgate, Hoccleve, Henryson; with William Caxton, father of English printing, and with John Gower, as fine a craftsman as ever turned a verse who is yet Langland's inferior in capacity. For all we know, Langland's family connections may have been a source of income to be added to his meager earnings as a cleric. An idea of a different order is to be drawn, however, from the motif of poverty that runs through the poem and helps with its dark threads to keep the poem cohesive. Surely the man who writes so knowingly and sympathetically about the condition of the poor and combines *pore* and *peple* in a formulaic phrase over and over again may well have experienced real poverty himself. It may be the only condition he knew from the day he was married until the end of his life.[5]

Through the twelve passus (ten in B) of the Visio, Langland builds consistently, if on a modest scale, with the three words *pore, riche,* and *syluer.* Beyond that point, as we have learned to expect, the additions in B multiply, depending on the theme of the various passus involved. Deletions in C are sufficiently numerous to suggest that, while the old poet has still his feelings of sympathy and regret regarding the spectacle and very odor of poverty, he is no longer inclined to react as he did when he wrote the B version and studded Passus XIV and XV in particular with an extravagance of two of the three words, *pore* and *riche.*

It may even be said that he has developed a kind of antipathy for the word *syluer* at the time of the C revision, as though the word had acquired an unpleasant connotation in becoming to him more and more a symbol of two evils, want and luxury. He deletes it twenty times, adds it only eight, but also uses *money* in five places where he might and probably would have used *syluer* in B.

There are twenty deletions in C as against eight additions. One question to be asked in this connection is why silver is so frequently mentioned and gold scarcely at all. (In C, it is actually devaluated almost out of sight—added once, deleted six times. It is added six times in B.)

Another question to be asked is why, in Passus XIV (on poverty) and Passus XV (on worldly priests and charity), Langland refers to the rich and to riches more frequently than to the poor and to poverty. In most of the patterns included in this study, the revisions in the C text are more revelatory in a biographical way than are those in B (for in C there comes, by implication, a summing up of values along with reappraisal of some values); but in the present pattern Langland tells us most about himself in the B version. Poets and pastors of the aristocracy might look down upon the suffering poor with genuine compassion, and in their compositions on the subject of poverty they would, and did, with nonparticipant objectivity speak of the strange and ragged creatures and the life in their squalid warrens.[6] The phenomenon of poverty, seen from a safe distance as a thing of dirt and patches, was described by them in terms befitting the subject, in what might be called the vocabulary of poverty—*want, hunger, privation, misery.*

Properly addressing himself to his topic, the outside observer would naturally confine his remarks to the various aspects of the phenomenon of poverty; and it would seldom occur to him, if at all, to bring in allusions to wealth and luxurious living. To someone enjoying security and all the comforts, poverty would be an unfortunate but distasteful condition. And normal optimism would dictate that it be considered briskly and briefly: held at arm's length and gingerly shaken, as it were, and then quickly put out of mind. The prosperous, that is, do not as a general thing spend a good part of their lives wistfully daydreaming about the blessings of an impoverished existence. When their thoughts take a primitivistic turn, they do not dwell on the simple tastes and belongings of the underprivileged in their community. The man caught fast in the toils of his civilization, surrounded by red tape, protocol, hierarchies of hierarchies, imagines himself translated through either a cultural or chronological change into an idyllic, simplified existence—one which is exotically in contrast with the fact of his way of life. When energy ebbs and problems multiply, the tropical island, the remote period in human history call to him. But it is a rare man of substance who escapes, either in thought or act, by sinking out of sight into the substratum of the poorest of the poor.

The true lower class, those born to a life of unrelieved privation, naturally have an attitude quite different from that of their social betters. Always in more desperate need of escape than their masters are in the worst of times, the poor and ignorant people turn their eyes upward and behold with never lessening fascination the magical existence of those who have what they themselves will never have. The spectacle of a brilliant society leisurely at play has a hypnotic effect on the underprivileged. In the Middle Ages, peasants' children played at being lords and ladies; the manners of great lords were imitated by their serfs in any small way possible, exactly as the manners of celebrities are emulated today. And always the victim of poverty would see his own hard life against the richly colored background of noble ease. In speaking of his own lot in life, he would, as a have-not, speak of what he lacked.

All of this discussion is a roundabout way of leading up to the topic of Langland's behavior when he undertook to discourse on the urgent theme of poverty. In making his allusions to wealth, he has the sound of an outsider looking in; his is the voice of a poor man who, in spite of his spirituality and awareness of transitory values, cannot help resenting the denial to his family and sometimes to himself of the good *things*. Incidence of the objective *riche* in its various forms seems to support Langland's statement that he was a poor man. He has shown in his delineation of Lady Meed how fully responsive he can be to external beauty, and it would seem that a man of his sensibilities and possibly genteel upbringing would have had the physical refinement and the necessary knowledge to appreciate the luxuries which please the senses and which he condemns so roundly. If so, his preoccupation with *riche* and its derivatives is the more understandable.

Langland's abiding concern for the poor has another, broader significance. The catholicity of his view of life and of humanity is evident from the time he first displays the field full of folk, and it is substantiated by many of the patterns in this study, among which the present pattern is to be counted. Here is further indication of Langland's personal poverty: his bias in favor of poor folk is not contrary to his desire to encompass the race if we consider that, in his humble world, he seldom encountered a man who was not to be called poor rather than rich. Even so, he does account for an inclusive cross section of humanity; but his heart is always turned toward his fellows in poverty, who probably are truly all the world to him much of the time. Again the very wide difference between the attitudes of Chaucer and Langland must be marked —Chaucer, the individualizer, presents some of his portraits in the habiliments of poverty but nowhere takes poverty as a theme; Langland, like Dostoyevsky in *Crime and Punishment,* makes endless thematic exploration.[7]

The following tabulations show, once again, the relative intensity of Langland's feelings in the B and C versions. Additions in B exceed by several times additions in C; deletions from A in B are scarcely to be found at all. Deletions from B are most numerous in the very passus which Langland had so heavily garnished with *riche* and *pore* in B. According to my count, *riche* is added as a single-word emendation only ten times in C and deleted even less. *Pore* and *syluer* are even more negligible as single-word emendations. The tables, consequently, are restricted to changes involving one or more lines.

Riche

Additions in B are: II—17, 77; III—268; IV—40; V—150; X—76, 83, 85, 96, 341, 344, 347; XI—185, 192, 288, 310; XII—76, 240, 245(2), 250, 261; XIII—439, 442; XIV—26, 73, 102, 104, 105, 123, 127, 132, 140, 144, 145, 148, 152(2), 157, 163, 168, 179, 182, 203, 204, 205, 206(2), 209, 210, 211, 212, 215, 220, 230, 291; XV— 79, 171(2), 172, 222, 228, 318, 325, 329(2), 333, 335, 336, 499, 500; XVII—259, 261, 265; XVIII—171, 208; XIX—69, 86, 280; XX—38, 180, 234.

Deletions from A: A II—62; X—113, 130.

Additions in C: III—184; IV—204, 327; V—153; VI—183; X—129, 134, 191(2); XI—261, 265; XIII—5, 26, 210, 226, 230(2), 247; XIV—5, 32, 58, 70, 80, 96, 98, 183; XV—19, 182, 185; XVI— 201, 233, 288, 308; XVII—21; XVIII—2, 212; XX—229, 233, 242; XXI—476.

Deletions from B: B III—207; IV—40; X—15, 96, 335, 336,

341, 344, 347; XI—192, 202, 310; XII—60, 250, 261; XIV—26, 73, 123, 127, 144, 145, 148, 152(2), 157, 168, 182, 211, 212; XV—171(2), 318, 325, 329(2), 333, 335, 336.

Pore

Additions in B: Prol.—90; I—173; III—240; V—157, 257, 258; VI—198; VIII—16; X—76, 80, 97, 347; XI—176, 178, 180, 189, 191, 202; XII—76; XIII—8, 78, 196, 301, 419, 425, 444; XIV—10, 26, 73, 108, 145, 174, 182, 194, 205, 207, 212, 220, 224, 225, 238, 244, 252, 259, 287, 289, 290, 291; XV—150, 178, 197, 241, 500; XVI—8; XX—233.

Deletions from A: A Prol.—93; II—62; X—113.

Additions in C: III—186; IV—284; V—123, 153; VI—78; IX—144, 147; X—72; XIII—164, 165; XIV—31, 99, 183; XV—16; XVI—201; XVII—3; XVIII—2.

Deletions from B: B V—257, 258; VI—198; VII—30; X—97, 347; XI—178, 202; XII—53; XIII—196, 301; XIV—10, 26, 73, 145, 182; XV—178, 197.

Syluer

Additions in B: Prol.—92, 168; I—101; II—67, 174; IV—30, 34, 130; V—95, 266; VI—195; IX—90; X—337, 361; XI—74, 168, 189, 217, 268, 274, 278; XIV—249, 268; XV—7, 79, 120, 123, 127, 235, 342; XVI—143; XVII—75, 264; XIX—369; XX—12, 221, 365.

Additions in C: I—164; IV—109, 392; V—51; VI—72; IX—248; X—119; XIII—17; XVI—36, 168; XVIII—74.

Deletions from B. B II—174; IV—30, 34; V—95, 266; VI—195; VII—206; IX—90; X—337, 361; XI—74, 168, 217, 268; XV—7, 120, 235; XVI—143; XVII—75.

IX Teche

Langland's satiric poem is completely didactic; there is no doubt that his strongest passion was for teaching. He probably acquired experience in preaching and teaching before the first page of *Piers Plowman* was begun; he certainly learned much during the writing of the poem and became a more resourceful teacher as a result; and, when it was finished, he read it to willing listeners and, as the best peddler the poem could have, probably sold copies of parts of it. Now, the person whose forte is teaching is either an egomaniac or a humanitarian, or both. A teacher whose lesson always relates to the single theme of grace and salvation would appear to be more interested in others than in himself, for the story he would tell is not his own but a very old one and is not to be paraded as his discovery or invention. He would feel an urgency of which the common folk seemed unaware and would try to impart some of his feeling, and that would be his contribution. In Langland's case, that was his life's work, and call it what one will—proselytizing, practical Christianity, missionary work—a passionate humanitarianism definitely belongs in the list.

As a source of evidence of a higher degree of intensity or enthusiasm in B, the pattern of *teche* (and *techynge, techour, tauʒte*), meaning both "teach" and "direct," conforms to the patterns of *al, wikked, riche, pore, syluer,* and oaths. Langland is especially carried away in Passus B XV and XIX; but in the parallel passus in C the additions are very light (three in XVII) or there are none (XXII), and deletions are numerous (seven from B XV, two from B XIX). B XV is an instruction by Anima on Charity. B XIX is a discourse by Conscience on the Church and the life of Christ. There are passages in *Piers Plowman* in which the device of repetition is used to such an extreme (*al, pore, riche, teche*) that there is obviously more involved than a mere rhetorical exercise—there is no mistaking the rise of fervency in these lines.

Additions and deletions consisting of very short emendations are scarce—thirteen additions in C and three deletions from B in the entire poem. For a clear contrast between A and B, the line references will therefore be limited to changes which occur in longer units (one line at least). To repeat, subconsciously motivated word choice is perhaps more clearly traceable in these longer units. The large totals in the B version have some significance, but as usual it is vitiated by the originality of B, which insures a higher incidence of almost *any* form in the last ten passus of B. In the first ten passus (twelve in C), the count is five additions in C against eleven in B; in the last half of the poem, fourteen in C against forty-two in B.

Whereas the old man was apparently *simpatico* in a most catholic sense, the additions and deletions of *teche* indicate that in the years when a man's powers are at the fullest Langland was less willing to indulge his foolish and wicked brothers and sisters; instead, he hoped to reform them. Teaching was, perhaps, a more urgent mission in his middle years than it was at the end.

Teche (and derivatives)

Additions in B are: III—221; V—12; VI—6, 224, 229; VII—74, 75; VIII—56; IX—93, 199; X—82, 203, 270, 338, 384, 405; XI—220; XII—37, 66, 109, 285; XIII—115, 116(2); XIV—25, 183; XV—67, 91, 93, 277, 400, 427, 494, 518, 563, 575, 577; XVII—27, 40, 116, 127, 147, 335; XVIII—227, 349; XIX—44, 165, 177, 228, 233, 266, 313, 357, 470; XX—8, 9, 119, 252, 300.

Deletions from A: A I—79 (Kane *Kenne*), 127 (Kane *Kenne*); II—31 (Kane *deest*); VII—215; X—95; XI—162; XII—2, 97.

Additions in C: I—120; II—145; IV—145; XI—101, 199; XIII—97; XVI—170; XVII—233, 241, 341; XVIII—78, 83, 174, 180, 254, 297; XIX—2, 138; XX—245.

Deletions from B: B I—109; III—252; VI—224, 229; VII—74, 75; X—151, 195, 203, 221, 268, 270, 338; XII—37; XIII—116; XIV—25; XV—67, 91, 277, 427, 494, 563, 575; XVII—40, 116, 147; XVIII—349; XIX—182, 233; XX—252.

One other pattern, a minor but striking one, is of the unifying symbolic type. It is not intertextual. Through seventy-six lines (B XVII, 203–79; C XX, 167–261) Langland symbolizes the Trinity with a torch brightly flaming; then, thirty-six lines later, he makes a transition into the topic of man's wickedness by using smoke as a symbol. Both symbols are maintained through a total of one hundred and eleven lines to the end of the passus. On line 124 of the following passus the symbol of light resumes, this time as the joy of the birth of Christ. The following are samples from the three symbolizations.

> And to a torche or a tapre the Trinitee is lykned;
> As wex and a weke were twyned togideres,
> And thanne a fyre flaumende forth oute of bothe;
> And as wex and weyke and hote fyre togyderes
> Fostren forth a flaumbe and a feyre leye,
> So doth the sire and the sone and also *spiritus sanctus*
>   (B XVII, 203–8)

Ac the smoke and the smolder that smyt in owre
    eyghen [eyes],
That is coueityse and vnkyndenesse that quencheth
    goddes mercy.   (B XVII, 341–42)
Eyther axed other of this grete wonder,
Of the dyne [din] and of the derknesse and how the
    daye rowed [dawned],
And which a liȝte and a leme [glow] lay befor helle.
                (B XVIII, 122–24)

CHAPTER 4

A Small Gallery

NO allegory in English has been explained with such reverent thoroughness by so many eminent specialists as has *Piers Plowman*. Coming late in the day as a critic of the poem and, late or early, being neither scriptural exegete nor theologian nor historian, I can best serve my reader by sending him to scholars who fit these descriptions. They are surprisingly divergent in their views, and there is a wide variation in the degrees of emphasis which they place on the importance of allegory; but their combined effort is a massive analysis that seems to me to leave little unsaid. If there is unbroken ground, it is where conditions and events in Langland's time need to be specifically related to the poem.

But the present book is primarily an introduction, and for allegory that is at once vivid, profound, and to a modern student comprehensible, the Seven Deadly Sins and Lady Meed and Lady Holychurch are the inevitable choices. "Unbroken ground" is certainly no description of the Seven Deadly Sins. Langland's characterizations follow an old tradition and are, moreover, never neglected by his commentators. He wields allegory in his attacks on all of the satirist's conventional targets and even, as in the case of Lady Meed, makes of it a blade to cut away the exterior and to expose potential evil within; for she is not, in her earliest state, reprehensible. Meed must exist in any constructive society. Bribery is another matter.

As I have already said, the allegory is seen at its most obscure when Piers is metamorphosed. It is extremely abstruse when Dowel, Dobet, and Dobest, whose very names personify them, are spoken of in most indefinite terms as participants; yet all the while what they actually represent is the general condition of right-living.

Not surprisingly, they have been interpreted in a number of ways. But then the entire poem takes on different shapes as seen by its many critics—surely the most dissident group of scholars in existence (Cf. Chapter I, note 17). For example, Robert W. Frank, Jr., believes that the poem may be profitably read on the literal level.[1] G. R. Owst, in his concern with pulpit literature, restricts himself to homiletics and sociological significance.[2] The three lives, Dowel, Dobet, and Dobest, though misread by some as simple progression, are explained by more thoughtful scholars, notably H. W. Wells[3] and Nevill K. Coghill,[4] as the active life, the contemplative life, and the mixed life.

On the subject of types of salvation, much disagreement clouds the air. If I may generalize crudely, Father T. P. Dunning,[5] Morton W. Bloomfield,[6] and Willi Erzgräber[7] view Everyman as protagonist; but E. Talbot Donaldson[8] and Elizabeth Zeeman Salter[9] represent a point of view which holds that the *mystic's* salvation is Langland's theme. In a study of the Scriptural traditions in the poem, D. W. Robertson, Jr., and Bernard F. Huppé work on the four familiar levels: literal, tropological, allegorical, and anagogical, defined thus: "The tropological meaning was that which applied to the individual so that it was frequently moral in application. The allegorical sense was used originally to interpret the Old Testament in the light of the New, or to interpret it as it applies to the Church. The anagogical sense is concerned with the heavenly mysteries." [10]

With the authorities not so much in warlike disagreement as in different schools, it should not be gravely injudicious to suggest to the beginner, who presumably will not be intent on breaking every crumb of meaning, that he take his profit and pleasure from *Piers Plowman* as he finds them. The Bible before and modern poetry long after have been read in this way; and, if something less than total import is gained, there is consolation in the fact that no one at a distance of almost six centuries can hope to reach at once complete understanding of a poem of almost infinite complexity and peculiarly of its time. Dryden's fine phrase on Chaucer, "God's plenty," obtains here as well, though Dryden would have misconstrued Langland's metrics as being even more irregular than Chaucer's. There is a feast for one and all regardless of taste or special interest.

I *Lady Meed and Lady Holychurch*

Langland demonstrates that, if he had chosen fiction as his medium—stories of action and suspense—he might have taken his place beside Chaucer and Dickens in character delineation. His Lady Meed is second only to Criseide as the most fascinating female in medieval English literature. And she is "related" to the Whore of Babylon! [11] In her first appearance she follows Lady Holychurch, with whom the Dreamer has been engaged in a dialogue. When he first came upon Holychurch the Dreamer saw "A loueliche lady of lere [face] in lynnen y-clothid . . . her face . . . faire were" (C II, 3, 10). Holychurch is literal only in being lovely and fair of face, clothed in linen, and talkative—as behooves her sex. Her allegorical level is far removed from the very literal allegory in which Lady Meed first appears.

If we contrast Meed's description with that of Holychurch, the richness of Meed's apparel is exciting to the eye; the effect is heightened because it is so unexpected.[12] To turn and behold a woman of great beauty dressed like the richest of queens is dramatic, but how much more so when the beholder is not only completely surprised by her glittering presence but has just been told that in the spot where she stands he would see the-three-who-are-one, False, Favel, and Liar, who might be guessed to be opposites to the magnificence of her Ladyship. These lines are the beginning of her portrait:

> I loked on my left half as the lady [Holychurch]
>   me taughte,
> And was war of a womman wortheli yclothed,
> Purfiled [furred] with pelure [fur] the finest vpon erthe,
> Y-crounede with a corone the kyng hath non better.
> Fetislich hir fyngres were fretted with golde wyre,
> And there-on red rubyes as red as any glede,
> And diamantz of derrest pris and double manere safferes,
> Orientales and ewages [beryls] enuenymes to destroye.
> Hire robe was ful riche of red scarlet engreyned,
> With ribanes of red golde and of riche stones;
> Hire arraye me rauysshed suche ricchesse saw I neuere;
> I had wondre what she was and whas wyf she were.
>   (B II, 7–18)

In the C version, she is "enchantid," led into wrongdoing, by Favel and can be regarded with some sympathy. She is beset by knights, clerks, jurymen, summoners, sheriffs, beadles, bailiffs, brokers, foregoers, victuallers, advocates, and all "the route that ran a-boute Mede." Meed is therefore an appealing figure in the same way that any woman alone among men is appealing. She is not at all helpless, and yet a certain helplessness is assumed. Theology rather protectively argues that she is in danger of being "mastered" by False's "merry speech." [13]

Already Meed has lost dignity in the minds of Langland's audience. A lady as great as she had first seemed to be would not be thought by Theology or anyone else to be so susceptible to False's blandishments. She is to lose still more at a progressive rate, and the next occurrence seats her on a litter in a procession that is only less fantastic than the utterly grotesque parade of the Seven Deadly Sins. Her company are False and Favel, riding on jurymen and reeves; Civil (Civil Law) and Simony, riding on rectors and rich adulterers; notaries on poor provisors (preemptors of livings); summoners and sub-deans on lechers. The commissary draws the cart, and cheats and tricksters come running behind. Meed is "in the myddes"; she is on her way, she thinks, to her wedding, and this is her entourage; these lines are her epithalamion. A proud pavilion and ten thousand tents have been pitched for the occasion.

Though things may not be going as she would wish, her status has lost merely a few points, no more. Her trial is held in order to determine not what her punishment shall be for loving False but what kind of man will better suit her as husband. This abrogation of her own free choice in the matter could be cause for deep resentment, as perhaps it is; but Lady Meed is much too politic a creature to let it show. When the clerk and the justices console her, she *mildly* thanks them all "Of hure grete goudnesse" and gives them cups of gold and silver, ruby rings, "and other riche ʒiftes," and to the humblest man of her company a gold coin. Again the lavishness of her nature has been borne out, and it begins to be apparent that her wealth and the power accruing from it are more impressive than her principles. The next incident leaves no doubt. A friar-confessor tells her that, although learned and ignorant men have lain with her and although False has "kept" her for forty

years, he, the friar, will absolve her for a seam of wheat. Langland's adverb for the delivery of this blunt speech, which is as
terse in the poem as in my summary, is *mildly* (C IV, 39), the
word used just above when Meed was talking. Her *mildly* loses
some of its benevolence from association with this ironic one.

Meed's answer to this offer is simply to kneel. After her confession, the friar asks her to provide funds for a church window; and
she laughs "louelich" and agrees. Her next speech, with the impatience of the Wife of Bath to get to her favorite topic, is testimo-
nial for and defense of lechery, on which she dwells for several
lines, obviously savoring the topic. Again the C text (only) has
mildly (1. 77).

She is summoned by the King and greeted courteously. When
the King asks her if she will marry Conscience, she assents, saying
"Lord forbid" she should answer otherwise. The oath "Lord forbid," like *mildly*, is at once turned against her when Conscience
answers "Lord forbid" that he should marry her. Her dignity is
shaken, as before, but she carries on, and does so in the face of
further insult. Conscience, framing his remarks like the shepherds'
in the *Secunda Pastorum*, goes on to say:

> "Er ich wedde suche a wif wo me by-tyde!
> For hue is freel of hure faith and fikel of hure speche . . .
> And lereth hem to lecherie that louyeth here ʒyftes . . .
> Ys nauht a betere baude by hym that me made!
> By-twyne heuene and helle alle erthe thauh me souhte.
> For hue is tykel of hure tail talewys [tale-bearing] of tonge,
> As comune as the cart-wey to knaues and to alle . . . etc.,
>   etc.," (157–68, for forty-seven lines more) [14]

If Meed is human, this attack will provoke more than a mild
response. Her anger does indeed grow as she speaks, beginning
with a reminder to Conscience of his past dependence on her and
proceeding through a record of her part in the King's wars. [15] She
accuses Conscience of having counseled the King (C IV, 242)
"caytiflyche" and "cowardliche" (B III, 205). She swears by Mary
and calls Conscience a pillager. So forceful is her rebuttal and so
logical is its consistency of theme—the necessities of meed for
granting of meed—that the moment she pauses (after sixty-five
lines) the King declares her to be worthy of victory.

There follows a long disquisition by Conscience on meed and mercede—bribery and just reward. In a marvelous verse Meed's temper is sharpened: "As wroth as the wynd wex Mede ther-after" (C IV, 486). Her answer, this time, is an incomplete Latin motto, *Honorem acquirit qui dat munera* (C IV, 489), which Conscience quickly corrects and completes, agreeing that the giver of meed acquires honor but adding the unwelcome reversal (to Meed) *animam autem aufert accipientium*—the receiver of meed is receiver of guile. Conscience has the last word, and Lady Meed has one more humiliation. Shortly thereafter she "meekens" herself in pleading for clemency for Wrong, a man close to her heart.

She is not yet crushed, however. Reason, who, like Conscience, is long of wind, delivers himself of a rather sententious tirade against Wrong and Meed, concluding with some Latin phrases that leave the clerks puzzling together.

Mede in the mote-halle tho [then] on men of lawe gan wynke,
In sygne that thei sholde with som sotel speche
Reherce tho a-non ryght that myghte Reson stoppe.
(C V, 148–50)

But she fails utterly to find support, and in her blackest hour she grieves with a heavy countenance; for, as Langland says, "the comune called hure queynte comune hore," using word-play to brand her with the obscenely ambiguous "queynte," and make her more common than any commoner. This is the end of the debate, and Lady Meed, the loser, steals softly out of the hall, accompanied by a juryman and a summoner.

Through all of Passus III and IV the personality, ideas, the policies of Lady Meed have unfolded in the comments of the narrator and in the dialogues between Meed and the other characters. The proud creature has attracted the pity of the "many" and has been entertained with "myrthe and mynstralcy" (C IV, 12) on her way to Westminster for the hearing. "Confortynge hure as thei couthe" (C IV, 16), certain justices have told her not to grieve or be sorrowful. If the reader feels something for her besides contempt, presumably what he feels will be pity.

In one of Langland's more obscure ironies, an added response is elicited by femininity; but this time Meed is not the subject. The previously mentioned symbolic contrast between Holychurch's and Meed's items of clothing does not represent the sole distinction to be made between the two. That it represents the main one—purity and austerity against the corruption of luxury—is obvious; but Langland's making of Holychurch a warmly human character *through* the familiar device of highly emotionalized dialogue is also a distinction. Meed has shown herself alert, resourceful, informed—illogical (not in a feminine way) only when distortion served her purposes; and her capacity for feeling anger, if nothing else, is well demonstrated. There is no suggestion of personal warmth, however; even her lust is completely promiscuous and depersonalized. If silence is an indication, she is indifferent to the rivalry of the other great lady.

Not so Holychurch. When the Dreamer first spies Meed and asks her name, the reply is quick and heated. Says Lady Holychurch, "That ys Mede the mayde . . . that hath noyed me ofte . . ." (C III, 19). She goes on to speak unkindly of Meed's parentage. Then, in a tone of resentment which is peculiarly feminine, using exactly the words a woman would use in her circumstance, she says, no doubt with chin and eyebrows raised:

"Ich ouhte be herre [higher] than hue. Ich kam of a betere,
The fader that me forth brouhte *filius dei* he hoteth, [is called]
That neuere lyede ne lauhwede in al hus lyf-tyme.
Ich am hus dere douheter duchesse of heuene. . . ."
                                                (C III, 30–33)

One point to be marked is that she is not "higher" than Meed in their society; yet, in her kindly willingness to instruct the inquisitive Dreamer and in her womanly outburst at Meed's undeserved popularity, she is incomparably the more attractive personage of the two. And so should she be, a gracious lady with a warm heart who is also Holy Mother Church. As an embodiment of qualities most desirable in a woman, she shines brightly if briefly in the poem and places Meed in the shadow that is deficiency.

Throughout Meed's struggles against Conscience and Reason, the King has proved interesting mainly because of his too human indecisiveness and his eagerness to settle the matter as amicably as possible; but, at the same time, he displays no real concern for the moral vaues at stake. B. F. Huppé, writing of the King in the framework of the entire poem, has said of him that he is wavering and irresolute; he has a temper, but little consistent will; he is vacillating and easily influenced.[16]

The behavior of the King during Lady Meed's three passus confirms Huppé's judgment perfectly. When the King first learns of the contemplated marriage between Meed and False, he orders the arrest of False with the intention of hanging him by the neck, strong punishment for an offender who is merely an overly ambitious suitor; and he issues this order with oaths and other strong phrases, roundly condemning the malefactors and sounding, indeed, like a true king in high dudgeon. The result of this sweeping command is hardly what His Majesty had ordered. Advised to flee, False "flegh to the freres" (III, 220); and Liar, lacking a welcome anywhere else, lets himself be drawn into the house of the pardoners. Neither refuge is sanctuary in the ecclesiastical sense, but so ineffectual is the King's authority that the fugitives are safe to the point of being free to come and go. The crisis is permitted to blow over.

As Passus IV opens, the King is issuing another of his royal pronouncements. First he puts Meed at her ease; then "Ich shal asaye hure my-self" (IV, 5) he says; and, if she heeds the counsel of wise men, "Ich wolle for-gyue hure alle hure gultes" (8). He ends with another resounding oath "so me God helpe!" (8), but it is an emphatic verbal seal on a resolution that only reveals him to be shallow in conviction, short in memory of injustices, and all too willing to come to terms with a thoroughly disreputable character. Confident of the King's tractability, the justices blandly assure Meed that they will influence the King and obtain *carte blanche* for her. In view of the fact that these justices are the "wise men" to whom the King has directed Meed for counsel, the King's ability to choose his ministers is put in serious doubt.

The King's ultimatum and the confession which Meed makes to the friar have not the slightest effect on her subsequent conduct, which is worse, if possible, than her record before the trial, her newest offense being the corrupting of the mayor himself. The King still regards her attachment for False as her worst offense, however. A second time she is hailed before him for a good scolding. "The lenger ich lete the go," he says, "the lasse treuthe ys with the" (IV, 136). If she does any further injury to himself and Truth, she will, "by Seint Marye my lady," be closed up in a dungeon as an anchorite and as a warning to all wanton women.

Meed makes her defense with strength and dignity, and the King is completely won over. The same cannot be said of Conscience, and, in the course of his argument against Meed, he instructs the King, who listens humbly, in the duties of the crown, the evils inherent in Meed, and the great power and importance of Reason. The King—having asked questions which stem from his ignorance and having listened in meek silence to a protracted definition of kingship and, to all appearances, having learned much from the lecture—arrives at a most surprising solution. It is nevertheless characteristic of him. "Kiss and make up," is what, in effect, he says to Meed and Conscience. "Serve me together." Conscience *not* surprisingly refuses at once with indignation, and demands that Reason be consulted. The King, who quickly assents, summons Reason to appear as witness. Of their meeting we are told only that they "speken tho [then] wise wordes a long while to-gederes" (V, 44).

Suddenly attention swings from Meed to Wrong. Here the King acts decisively and, despite the pleas of Meed and Peace in Wrong's behalf, declares that, unless Reason takes pity on Wrong, that worthy shall rest in the stocks as long as the King lives. Though Wrong, an allegorical expansion, embodies Meed, as well as other sins or occasion of sin, he by no means receives from the King the sympathetic consideration bestowed upon Meed. It is true that the King, true to pattern, is in part avoiding his responsibility by passing the job of the ultimate judging to Reason. The result is foregone, however. In his first words Reason makes clear that Wrong will never be condoned by him.

I believe that Langland, who presents himself in all three versions as a loyal subject and supporter of kinghood, has found kings to be mortal and fallible but staunchly aligned on the side of Right, and this is his message. His King resembles most Edward III. In the C version, although at the time it was made Edward III was long dead, the sketch of the King stands unaltered. Together Passus III, IV, and V are lengthened by over twenty-five per cent in C, but the passages relating directly to the King are not the extended parts. Langland's increased interest and skill in characterization are illustrated in the fuller treatment in C of minor characters.

II *The Seven Deadly Sins*

A small amount of Passus VII and VIII, which set forth the Seven Deadly Sins in Rabelaisian personifications, is actually deleted in the C version. If my discussion of some of the features of Langland's portraits were to be limited to C, it would still be impossible to pay equal attention to all the details in Langland's gallery of grotesques. For the sake of economy, I shall extract some of the most pungent, comic, and epigrammatic lines and thereby hope to advance the cause of this book—the awakening of modern readers with interests mainly in the more modern periods of literature to certain qualities in Langland's work which are timeless and which serve as evidence of his rightful place among the greatest of English poets.

The Seven are to appear in a rather peculiar setting, for the stage is their confessional; and, as each comes forward, somewhat in the manner of the cast in *Everyman,* the audience understands that, if the truth concerning him is ever to be learned from his own lips, now is the moment. The theme of confession and repentance is germane to the passus just finished in which Meed and Wrong came close to strict sentencing. Wrong, a very general abstraction, is composed of all the types of sin, and in C VII Langland proceeds with the individualization of seven of the components of which Wrong is made up.

a PRIDE

Pride is traditionally first in the list of the Deadly Sins. Pernell Proud-heart throws herself to the ground, lies there a long while, then looks up and "Lord, mercy, criede" (VII, 4) and promises God that she will put on a hairshirt; but she is not reported as actually putting on such a shirt. Speaking directly to an age of competition, the twentieth century, she admits to competitiveness, to her practice of scorning the skills of others and of willing that men judge her to be "konnyngest of my craft" (VII, 42). By her own account, she is a busy talker who usually lies. When she keeps the facts straight, she is telling of something like her latest alms-giving; but even then she has to worry about being believed. And so at this time she says to "suche that sytten me by-syde,"

"Lo, yf ȝe leyue me nouht other [or] that ȝe wene ich lye,
Aske of hym other of hure and thei conne ȝow telle
What ich soffrede and seih and som tyme hadde,
And what ich knew and couthe and what kyn ich kam of."
                                              (VII, 54–58)

The verbosity of Pride is also evident in this redundant string of
generalities, and may be one of Langland's reasons for casting this
sin as a woman. Traditionally, the vice had more often been cast
as a male (the devil, kings, princes) than as a female.

b ENVY

The portrait of Envy is drastically cut in C; consequently, my
excerpts are from B. In B (and in A), Envy, lacking that which
nourishes Pride, is "pale as a pelet [white stone]" and "in the
palsye he semed" (B V, 78). The former of these traits is in the
tradition of allegorized envy.[17] Envy is debilitating, a drain of
one's energies; and palsy may be taken here as a symptom of
weakness. Envy's unhealthy pallor is further illustrated in a simile
more striking than the first one: ". . . as a leke hadde yleye long
in the sonne so loked he with lene chekes lourynge foule" (B V,
82–83).

Though his cheeks are lean, his body is swollen with gall; and,
though his stout body is weak, he goes about energetically wring-
ing his hands, seeking revenge. "Al his curteysye" (B V, 90) is
chiding and challenging and backbiting with "an addres tonge"
(87). Even his prayers in church are vengeful. As competition was
Pride's favorite theme, vengeance is Envy's. Where Pride was a
success, Envy is a failure; and, as a consequence of his misfortune
in life, he is full of self-pity. A real hypochondriac, he goes on at
great length about his sufferings:

"Whenne ich ne may haue the maistrie such malencolie ich take,
That ich cacche the crampe the cardiacle som tyme,
Other [or] an ague in such an angre and som tyme a feuere . . ."
                                              (C VII, 77–79)

He may not eat as others do, not even sweet things. It is necessary
for Repentance to interrupt him, so engrossed has he become in

cataloguing the causes of his unhappiness. "Be [thow] ryght sory / For thy synne . . . ?" asks Repentance. With humor more bitter than he realizes, Envy's answer is completely in character: "Ich am euere sory, ich am bote selde other; / That [is what] maketh me so megre for ich ne may me auenge" (C VIII, 93–94). He grumbles on, preoccupied as ever with his frustrations. At last he catches himself, and in two hasty, stereotyped lines he asks the Lord for grace of amendment.

c WRATH

Wrath, who is next, "awakens" (C VII, 103)[18] "With a nyuy-lynge nose" which undoubtedly helps to keep him irritable; and he is "nyppyng hus lyppes," too frustrated to snap like a turtle. Even coming after the strong words of Pride and Envy, the violence of his expression is a shock. In the first five lines his intensity is frightening as he speaks of stalking, of smiting with stone and staff, and of thinking up sleights the better to slay his enemy. In seven years, he says, he could not tell all the harm he has done "with hand and with tonge" (C VII, 109). If he is given some sisters in a convent, he will have them screaming "You lie" at one another; and then in the excitement he himself will "crie and cracche [scratch] with my kene nailes, / Bothe byte and bete . . ." (140–41). Another frenzied scene of the type Wrath loves is created when he attends Mass with some wives and widows and goes to breakfast, with two of them apparently. Then in his own words

> ". . . ich, Wratth, was . . . wroth on hem both,
> Til aither cleped other 'hore' and of [off] with the clothes,
> Til bothe here heuedes were bar and blody here chekes."
>   (C VII, 148–50)

Oddly, when Wrath gets among men—or monks, to be exact—instead of kindling them to anger, as with the women, he is chastised for telling tales (probably in attempts to provoke the monks), made to dine on bread and water, whipped "on the bar ers" (C VII, 157). Earlier in his monologue, however, he has attacked friars as well as "beggars and barouns" (123). At the same time, he has expressed his distaste for the austerity of the monks'

mode of life and yet has made the passing comment on nuns that
"Hem were leuere swouny other swelte [die] than suffry eny
peyne." (C VII, 129). All in all there is a hint of antifeminism.
Langland is not the first to suggest that women's tongues and tem-
pers are worse than men's.

Wrath's only word of regret has to do with "a flux of a foul
mouth" (C VII, 161) that follows his drinking bouts. Repentance
absolves him perfunctorily and bids him pray for God's help.

d   LECHERY

Wrath, then, was steeped in his "humour" and never drew a
breath that was not an angry breath, never softened. Lechery
makes himself distinct from Wrath with the first word he speaks—
"Alas!" (C VII, 170). Langland's understanding of the complex
nature of guilt, the difference between the effects on conscience of
two types of sin, is well illustrated by Lechery's remorse, following as it does Wrath's refusal or inability to recognize his own
guilt. "Alas!" is the beginning of a prayer to "oure lady" to inter-
cede with her Son, and this petition is followed by a promise to
"Drynke bote [but] with the douke and dyne bote ones [once]"
(174). Soon Lechery's confession takes a voluptuous turn; and,
like many another, including Lady Meed before him, he goes with
relish into unnecessary details:

> "To eche maide that ich mette ich made hure a sygne
> Semynge to synne-warde and somme gan ich taste
> A-boute the mouthe, and by-nythe by-gan ich to grope,
> Til oure bothers wil was on; to werke we ʒeden [went]
> As wel fastyngdaies as Frydaies and heye-feste euenes,
> As luf [lief] in lente as oute of lente alle tymes liche—
> Suche werkus with ous were neuere out of seson—
> Til we myghte no more; thanne hadde we murye tales
> Of puterie [lechery] and of paramours and proueden
>   thorw speches,
> Handlynge and halsynge [embracing] and al-so thorw
>   cussynge,
> Excitynge oure aither other til oure olde synne;
> Sotilede [invented] songes and sende out olde baudes
> For to wynne to my wil wommen with gyle;
> By sorcerye som tyme and som tyme by maistrye.
> Ich lay by the louelokeste and loued hem neuere after.

> Whenne ich was old and hor and hadde lore [lost]
>   that kynde [nature],
> Ich had lykynge to lauhe of lecherous tales."
>   (C VII, 178–94)

He ends with a second prayer for mercy.

e AVARICE

Avarice fails to bring forth a statement of repentance, but he does acknowledge his sins. As a penitent, he is, then, less successful than Envy, to whom he bears close relationship. Like Envy, he can turn a joke against himself and does so—in fact, more often with plays on words that are made more knowingly than Envy's. Next to Glutton, Avarice is the portrait most lightened by the element of humor; even his description is built on ridiculous exaggerations:

> Thenne ca[m] [19] Couetyse ich can nat hym discryue,
> So hongerliche and so holwe Heruy hym-self lokede.
> He was bytelbrowed and baberlupped with two blery eyen,
> And as a lothcrenc pors lollid hus chekus,
> Wel sydder [lower] than hys chyn ychiueled [trembled]
>   for elde:
> As bondemenne bacon hus berd was yshaue,
> With hus hod on his heued and hus hatte bothe;
> In a toren tabarde of twelue wynter age;
> But ʒif a lous couthe lepe I leue hit, as y trowe,
> He scholde not wandre on that welch [cloth] so was hit
>   threde-bare.   (C VII, 196–205) [20]

Appropriately, Avarice is lean of face, like Envy; and his ragged beard above a ragged coat is a symbol of want. Garbing him shabbily because he is always in need makes for a sharpness of irony unusual even in Langland: Avarice finds prey among all classes *except* the poor, whose level of subsistence is so low that coveting of superfluities is unthinkable—the poor think only of finding enough food to keep soul and body together. To the navvy today, after two centuries of social reforms in the West, his glass of mild is not only his greatest luxury but, because it is higher in food value than most of the solids he consumes, is also an essential source of energy. John Lawlor, in his discussion of poverty in

Piers Plowman, refers to Passus XVII, the passage where Avarice finds it impossible to grapple with Poverty, "a pety thyng" who hardly reaches to the navel of Avarice. Here, says Lawlor in one of his provocative (and subjective) speculations, "we seem to catch an echo of sporting sentiment for the wily little man matched against a gigantic adversary. The comic disproportion answers to the inherent impossibility of any real bout in these terms. . . ." [21]

The confession scene contains other gleams of Langland's sardonic humor on the subject of avarice and also some masterly strokes of characterization. In the broad view, the mode of life followed by Avarice resembles the precarious living-by-wits of a confidence man, and the reader recognizes the type instantly and smiles at him. He is the prototype of all those fascinating scoundrels who people literature as well as the real world—Chaucer's Canon and his yeoman, Lazarillo and the other picaros, Jonson's Subtle, Voltaire's Candide, and Dickens' wide array. We laugh and disapprove at the same time, and even when a great personage playing a serious part (the Green Knight) manages very neatly to engineer a deception, the reaction of the audience is one of amusement. Secretly, we approve skulduggery of a fairly harmless order and admire the nonconforming type who slips past convention and law and uses a new trick to make a profit. The recent "robbery" of a Montgomery, Alabama, bank by a used-car dealer (also part-time gambler) proves the immutability of human nature. Through an error, $43,000 was deposited to his account. He promptly withdrew it in cash, put the money somewhere out of reach of the bank and police, and then argued that several long-standing gambling debtors might have paid him through his bank account and caused the change in his bank balance just before the time of the withdrawal. Since no intention to commit a crime can be fixed on him, he is presumably safe from prosecution. His fellow townspeople, bank officers excluded, have *una voce* praised, reassured, and joshed him; by practical standards *he is a richer man in more ways than one.*

"I first learned to lie, then to give false measure of everything I sold," says Avarice. His recitation, like Envy's, shows him so busy in wrongdoing that Repentance must interrupt—emphatically, for even he is shocked. "Repentest thow neuere?" quath Repentaunce / "ne restitucion madest?" (C VII, 234). The reply is a rico-

cheting pun off the word *restitucion*. It is also the beginning of
one of Langland's liveliest dialogues. Yes, he once made restitution when "a hep of chapmen . . . a reste were" (236). He rifled
their luggage!

Repentance tells Avarice that he will hang "here or in hell" for
that kind of restitution; then he ventures another question, this
time concerning usury. Only in youth, it seems, did Avarice practice usury. Whether he did so over a period of one year or ten he
does not say. Repentance interrupts his list of some of the loans he
had made as a usurer: "Lenedest thow euere to eny lorde for
loue of menteynaunce?" (248). The reply: Yes, but they "louede
me neure after" (249).

Repentance tells him that he simply must make restitution. Toward the end of another long list of swindles, Avarice does get
around to the matter of church and sin; but he does so only within
his distorted conception of both. When in church, instead of beg-
ging mercy for misdeeds, he spent the time thinking, he says,
about goods that had got away from him; instead of dread of his
deadly sins, he dreaded loss of his goods. This situation reminds
us of the time when Envy was in church and his thoughts cen-
tered on the theft of his bowl and torn sheet. Avarice's greediness
is marked in debate as in business: we have seen how he seizes
the other's words and twists them to please himself.

Repentance is exasperated with him and among other uncom-
plimentary remarks uses an earthy expression more typical of the
C version than of A or B: ". . . an hore of hure [her] ers-
wynnynge may hardiloker [more boldly] tythe / Than an erraunt
vsurer . . . / And erest [first of the two] shal come to
heuene . . ." (C VII, 306–8). The exchange ends with Repentance still urging Avarice to make amends.

ƒ GLUTTONY

Now to confession comes Glutton; of all of Langland's characters, he is the most vividly conceived and fully realized—and the
best known to Langland's audience through five and a half centuries. His name is the first mark of distinctiveness to be noted.
Quite naturally and perhaps without giving it too much attention
Langland would choose "Glutton" instead of "Gluttony." Of all
the Sins it is today the only one Lust included in which the ab-
stract noun names the perpetrator merely by dropping a suffix.[22]

As a result, the screen of allegory is dropped; and here is a man who is tagged like anyone else with a descriptive nickname. It is difficult for the reader to keep in mind that he is an allegorical figure.

Even after all we have seen of irony, humorous word-play, and slapstick comedy the account of Glutton dazzles from the first hemistich: "Now by-gynneth Gloton for to go to shryfte," (C VII, 350). He does not go; he *begins* to go—and the simple word foreshadows a long delay. He will confess, in time, but a monstrously disgusting scene must be enacted first. The second line puns on *coupe* [sin], anticipating the very climax, which should be anti-climax, of his debauch, when he rises up on his befouled bed and asks, "wher is the cuppe?" (A V, 213. B and C have *bolle*).

The processional continues in the second line: "And kayres hym to-kirke-ward hus coupe to shewe." Every phrase points to good intention and also to the merest beginning. He begins, not to confess, but to go, and not to go to confession or even to church, but only *toward* the church. In the third line of his sketch it comes again: "forth gan he wende." We see how perfect is his resolution, how complete his plan—a brew-wife asks him whither he is bound, and "To holy churche," quath he "for to hure masse, / And sitthen sitte and be yshriuen and synwe namore" (C VII, 355–56).

The man's duty is fully recognized. More or less hopeful of completing his mission, he gets himself into bustling motion. In the next breath, duty is forgotten. Asked if he will try some of her ale, he doesn't even bother to say "I don't mind if I do." Of course he will have the ale! He answers with "eny hote spices?": "Thenne goth Gloton yn and grete othes after" (361). The oaths are inspired by conviviality and a plenty of ale and spices.

Of the six other allegorical characters, the only one that approaches Glutton in sociability is Lechery. Pride, Avarice, Envy, and Wrath are exclusive by nature; and to a poet who loves the human race—all of it—these sins are bound to seem more intolerable than the sins, however selfish, that call for company. In a manner of speaking, lechery and gluttony are social vices. Therefore, it is not surprising that Glutton enters a company of thirty-six people (listed in order), plus a "heap" of second-hand furniture sellers, and that all of the motley crowd seem to hold him in good esteem.

As the description of Glutton continues, the details are the sort
Chaucer favored in treating of the Miller and the Merchant—
strictly physical. Yet there is a difference, as in almost everything
Langland touched. The highly distinctive features given to Avarice make firm in the memory the face of that character. One
would have expected Avarice to be narrow and mean of face, and
one is surprised by what appears instead. Langland must have
been familiar with grasping men whose eyes were bleared from
overseeing and whose cheeks were hollow but also ponderously
saturnine, heavy from the constant accretion of gathered goods. It
is the *face* of Avarice upon which Langland concentrates.

Now, before Glutton ever comes before the confessor Repentance, it should be easy to make guesses about his physiognomy
(like the gluttonous divine's in C XVI, 86 ff.): bulging cheeks;
eyes folded in fat; thick wet lips; general obesity. This description
is *too* easy. And so, since a glutton must look something like that,
the man having become what he is as a result of what he has drunk
and eaten (instead of showing the effect of a mental vice such as
Avarice's), Langland bothers not at all with some patient catalogue of a fat man's features. In its place, he reports the *movements* of the fuddled, besotted man and refers rather to the
functions of the body than to its appearance. (One lone clause,
"Gloton was a gret cherl," says anything at all about his size and
says exactly what should be taken for granted.) The device used
best by Rabelais and Swift is here brought into play—scatology to
an absolute extreme; and the fond eater and drinker who would
not be at least a little discouraged by Glutton's behavior must have
a hardy stomach indeed. Langland uses filth for the sake of reform, a simple equation that would be of immeasurable benefit to
most realistic writers today:

> Ther was lauhyng & lakeryng [chiding] and "let go the
>   coppe!"
> Bargeynes and beuereges by-gunne to aryse,
> And setyn so til euesong rang and songe vmbwhyle,
> Til Gloton hadde yglobbed a galon and a gylle.
> Hus guttes gonne godely [rumble] as two gredy sowes;
> He pissede a potell in a pater-noster-while,
> And blew hus rounde rewet [horn] atte rygbones ende,
> That alle that herde that horne hulde here nose after,
> And wusched hit hadde be wexed with a wips of breres.

He myghte nother stappe ne stonde tyl he a staf hadde.
Thanne gan he go lyke a glemannes bycche,
Som tyme asyde and som tyme a-rere,
As ho so laith lynes for to lacche foules.
And whenne he drow to the dore thanne dymmed hus
    eyen;
He thrumbled at the threshefold and threw to the erthe.
Tho Clement the cobelere cauhte hym by the mydel,
For to lyfte hym on loft he leyde hym on hus knees;
Ac Gloton was a gret cherl and gronyd in the liftynge,
And couhed vp a caudel in Clementes lappe;
Ys non so hongry hounde in Hertforde-shire,
That thorst [dares] lape of that leuynge so vnloueliche
    hit smauhte . . .   (C VII, 394–414)
That with al the wo of this world his wyf and his wenche
Beeren him hom to his bed and brouhten him ther-inne.
And after al this surfet an accesse he hedde,
That he slepte Saturday and Sonenday til sonne wente
    to reste.
Thenne he wakede of his wynk and wypede his eiȝen;
The furste word that he spac was "wher is the cupp?"
                   (A V, 208–13)

Bad as he is, Glutton is an occasional sinner; that is, he may sin once a day but not every waking hour of all of his days, as Envy and Avarice do. He has his clear moments, his periods of remission during which he sees with clarity the wages of self-corruption. He is thus able to make a good confession—the best of the lot, in fact—and to look when he is sober to possible salvation, and to do so with Langland's tentative blessing.

g   SLOTH

Shriving is in the air and, excepting Envy and Avarice, on the minds of all of the sinners. Morally sluggish Sloth comes straight to the point. In spite of his appearance ("al by-slobered with two slymed eyen" [C VIII, 1]) and his protestations of physical incapacity, he leads by his own account a fairly normal life and lacks initiative only in doing the Lord's work. His first syllables are comical, for he scarcely pronounces the word "shryuen" before he begins digressing about his favorite topic—fatigue. He opens with: "Ich most sitte to be shryuen." . . . Then he bethinks himself of his purpose and begins to bless himself, but he is as poor a beginner as Glutton. First Sloth belches, then stretches, and starts to snore.

Aroused by Repentance, he admits by implication that it is in the area of religion particularly that his energies fail, an admission that will strike a responsive chord in the audience. Ballads he remembers easily, but not the *pater-noster* or any vows he ever made or any penance the priest gave him. When he tells his beads, his thoughts are ten miles away. Yet he is a special case in this kind of dereliction, for one idea that Langland seems to wish to convey is that Sloth was formerly a priest himself, a magnified symbol of all careless worshippers.

Sloth certainly has an acute appreciation of sins of omission, and his recitation covers for the most part all the things he never did but should have done—visiting the sick, reading religious books, keeping Lent, learning his Latin (as a priest). He never could, he says, so much as understand another man's courtesy to him; furthermore, his manners might be called those of a hawk. And bad manners are indeed usually omissive.

It is notable that Langland, in maintaining a central theme which can be stated in the word *love*, moves closer to that center in portraying Sloth than he does in any of the other sketches. The intersection of the artery of the poem is of especial note since sloth is not one of the sins Langland regards as most deadly. But then the traditional seven, as Bloomfield has stated at length, are not all of them the most deadly of man's transgressions. Wanhope, or despair, may be the end of the slothful man, it is true, and Langland warns against it.[23] Nevertheless, to be guilty of slothfulness, or of any of the other six conditions enumerated by Langland, is not necessarily to be condemned irrevocably to hell. Sloth goes on to say that he is not "allured" by love (C VIII, 45). Whenever a fellow Christian does him a kindness, he forgets it sixty times; and he has often wasted good fish and flesh that might have gone to the poor.

With Pride and Envy, the recurring theme was competition; with Sloth it is his idle, suggestive tales. Although not all of Passus VIII is devoted to Sloth, there are within the passus nine occurrences of the topic of tales of "harlotrie" as an occasion of sin. Some of these are in Sloth's own phrases; as many again are part of a long discourse which is really the poet speaking. Minstrelsy and frivolous tales are obviously of real concern to Langland; and, as E. T. Donaldson has observed, Langland talks about minstrelsy more than does any other fourteenth-century poet.[24] If he seems puritanically narrow on the subject, the other extreme seen in today's permissive censors should be held up for comparison. Also there is the echo of Langland in Shakespeare's Sonnet 129 ("Th' expense of spirit in a waste of shame"), that matchless indictment of lust; and who will argue either that Shakespeare was a prude or that obsessive lust cannot cause decay of moral fiber?

Langland approaches the topic from a number of angles, ranging from balladry and alehouse tales to the blandishments of flatterers and to the stories told by harlots themselves. Sample quotations are:

> "With ydel tales atte nale [alehouse] and other-whyle in
> churches;
> Godes pyne and hus passion is pure selde in my
> thouhte . . ."   (C VIII, 19–20)

> "Ich hadde leuere huyre of harlotrye other of a lesyng
> [lie] to lauhen of,
> Other lacke men, and lykne hem in vnlykynge manere,
> Than al that euere Marc made Matheu, Iohan, other
> Lucas."   (C VIII, 22–24)

> And hath no lykynge to lerne ne of oure lord hure [hear],
> Bote harlotrie other horedom other elles of som wynnyng.
>   (C VIII, 75–76)

> Ry3t so flaterers and foles aren the fendes procuratores,
> Entysen men thorgh here tales to synne and to harlotrie.
>   (C VIII, 90–91)

> Sholde non harlot haue audience in halle ne in chaum-
> bre, . . .   (C VIII, 94)

> Clerkus and kny3tes welcometh kynges mynstrales,
> And for loue of here lordes lithen [hear] hem at festes;
> Muche more, me thenketh riche men auhte
> Haue beggers by-fore hem whiche beth godes myn-
> strales,
> As he seith hym-self seynt Iohan bereth witnesse,
> Qui uos spernit, me eciam spernit.

Ther-for ich rede ʒow riche reueles when ʒe maken
For to solace ʒoure soules suche mynstrales to haue;
The poure for a fol sage syttynge at thy table,
With a lered man, to lere the what oure lord suffrede
For to sauy thy saule fram Satan thyn enemye,
And fithele [fiddle] the, with-oute flateryng of goode
    Fryday the geste [story],
And a blynde man for a bordiour [jester] other a bed-
    reden womman
To crye a largesse by-fore oure lorde ʒoure goode loos
    [praise] to shewe.
Thuse thre manere mynstrales maken a man to lauhe;
In hus deth-deynge thei don hym gret comfort,
That by hus lyue litheth hem and loueth hem to huyre.
Thuse solaceth the soule til hym-self be-falle
In a wel good hope, for he wroghte so a-mong worthy
    seyntes;
Ther flaterers and foles with here foule wordes
Leden tho that lithen hem to Luciferes feste,
With *turpiloquio* [evil speaking], a lay of sorwe and
    Lucifers fithele,
To perpetuel peyne other purgatorye as wykke;
                       (C VIII, 97–118)

It will be seen that the first two of the above quotations are spoken by Sloth; the remainder come under Langland's general commentary. Here we have the first of two stages by which Langland moves outward from the specific sin of sloth through the larger area embracing all of the seven and at last to sin and repentance in a total view.

The gradual reentry into the world of individual sinners is also to be marked in the relationship between Repentance and Sloth and between Repentance and all the sinful. At the beginning of the passus, Repentance is ready and waiting for Sloth to make his confession; and Sloth immediately begins grumbling about feeling tired. The comic effect gained is augmented six lines later when Repentance tells Sloth, already dozing, to wake up and hurry to shrift and again some fifty lines later when a stern "Repente the-[e]" proves too much for Sloth's delicate resistance and he promptly swoons. Once more Repentance issues his command, but this time to the assemblage; and we know from the change that the transition has been made and that Sloth is no longer the sole and immediate concern of Repentance.

Perhaps one more remark should be made before the discussion of these seven allegorical characters is concluded. Of them all, Sloth is the one with whom Langland seems to identify. Like the Dreamer, in whom Langland must have put something of himself, Sloth speaks of the difficulty of stooping; and, while Sloth falls asleep in church, the Dreamer falls asleep on his way to church.

CHAPTER 5

Social Satire Broadly Aimed

CERTAIN foregoing pages may have seemed to suggest that Langland was in all aspects of his work an exceptional writer. The truth is that his social satire chooses the familiar targets—Fallen Man as a general theme, with specific treatments for clergy, doctors, lawyers, minstrels, and others. The proportions which he sets up are his own; but, while he pays more attention to the clergy than to any other types, there is nothing unusual in such an approach. It is probably in his inclusiveness, his exhaustive coverage of the multifarious walks of life within the professions, that his poem is individual. He never leaves off talking about them in the plural—deans, doctors, drapiers—and probably outdoes all other writers in his use of these plural designations.

In the very beginning of the poem we are shown the field ironically described as "fair." Lines added in C are an early hint that more evil than good is to be found in this field. The first of two positive words in the passage below—*welthe*—is far from representing any ideal of Langland's. The other word is *tryuthe*, and it is outweighed in the unbalanced comparisons in the third line:

> Al the welthe of this worlde and the woo bothe,
> Wynkyng as it were wyterly [truly] ich saw hyt,
> Of tryuthe and of tricherye of tresoun and of gyle,
> Al ich saw slepynge as ich shal ʒow telle.
>
> (C I, 10–13)

I *The Lower Orders*

The first impression of the field is that it is largely populated by the clergy. Before he finishes, Langland has surveyed them from the lowliest hermit to the Pope. Generally speaking, friars were probably the most blameworthy in real life, and they are kept under steady and heavy attack in *Piers Plowman*.[1] But let us begin with the hermits: "Eremytes on an hep [crowd] with hokede staues / Wenten to Walsyngham and hure wenches after" (C I, 51–52). The next line, "Grete lobies [lubbers] and longe that loth were to swynke," is so much like one of the Dreamer's statements about himself that Will indirectly identifies with these wastrels:

> "Ich am to waik to worche with sykel other [or] with sythe,
> And to long, leyf [believe] me lowe for to stoupe,
> To worchen as a workeman eny while to dure [endure]."
>   (C VI, 23–25. Not in A or B)

In a typical passage Langland distinguishes between "holy hermits" and

> . . . eremites that en-habiten by the heye weyes,
> And in borwes [boroughs] among brewesters and beggen
>   in churches;
> Al that holy eremytes hateden and despisede,
> As rychesses and reuerences and ryche mennes almesse,
> These lolleres, lacchedraweres [burglars] lewede eremytes,
> Coueyten the contrarie . . .   (C X, 188–93)

Pilgrims and beggars, some of whom no doubt considered themselves to have a religious calling, get their share of scolding. In one passage in the C version, irony is sacrificed for the sake of simple force. A and B have *wyse* and *wise* for *vn-wyse*, where the poet is saying of pilgrims and palmers that they "Wenten forth in hure way with meny vn-wyse tales, / And hauen leue to lye al hure lyf-time" (C I, 49–50).

What he says of *bydders* [beggars] and *beggers* is remembered a few lines later when he lists *mendinants* [mendicants] among the four orders of friars:

> Bydders and beggers faste a-boute ʒoden [went],
> Tyl hure bagge and hure bely were bretful [bread]
>   ycrammyd.
> Faytynge [shamming] for hure fode and fouhten atten
>   ale [ale-house].
> In glotenye, god wot goth they to bedde
> And aryseth with ribaudrie tho [those] Roberdes
>   [robber] knaues;
> Slep and synful sleuthe seweth [pursue] suche euere.
>   (C I, 41–46)

Summoners and sub-deans appear together in two different passages: "Somenours and southdenes that *supersedeas* [writs] taketh, / On hem that louyeth lecherie lepeth vp and rydeth, / On executores and suche men cometh softliche after" (C III, 187–89). In Passus XVII "somners and here lemmannes" are linked with "secutores [executors] and sodenes"; also with "imparfit preestes and prechers after seluer" (276–77).

A few lines prior to this there is an indictment of particular vividness in which hypocrisy is likened to a snow-covered dung-heap. Again priests and preachers are cast together; prelates dignify the company:

> Ypocrisie is a braunche of pruyde and most among clerkes,
> And is ylikned in Latyn to a lothliche dounghep,
> That were by-snywe al with snow and snakes with-ynne,
> Or to a wal whit-lymed and were blak with-inne.
> Ryȝt so meny preestes prechours and prelates,
> That beth enblaunched with *bele paroles* and with *bele* clothes;
> And as lambes thei loken and lyuen as wolues.
>
> (C XVII, 264–70)

We shall be meeting with prelates again as the survey of Langland's clergy takes us to the top of the hierarchy. But first other members of lower orders are to be accounted for.

When Liar is hooted out of houses and packed off because of the tales he has told, there is only one refuge for him—with the pardoners. In an imagined community of pardoners—or perhaps Langland means that Liar is adopted by one pardoner at a time, successively—he is pulled, not merely invited, "to house," washed and wiped and wound in clouts, and then sent with seals, or pardons, to church, where he is paid "pound-meel a-boute" (by pounds at a time). After he has been thus elevated, various laymen solicit his service.

The familiar pardoner is said to preach "as he a prest were": "He blessede hem [the ignorant] with hus breuet [letter of indulgence] and blerede hure eyen, / And raghte [seized] with hus rageman [papal bull] rynges and broches" (C I, 72–73). Pardoners are lumped together with parish priests: "The parsheprest and the pardoner parten the seluer" (C I, 79).

In one extraordinary passage which is at odds with his remarks

elsewhere, Langland eulogizes cloister and school as the only possible heaven on this earth. He also castigates monks and canons
who go into the world of commerce. The speaker is Reason:

> "Gregorie the grete clerk gart [caused] write in bokes
> The ruele of alle religious ryghtful and obedient.
> Right as fisshes in flod whenne hem faileth water,
> Deyen for drouthe whenne thei drye liggen,
> Ryght so religion roteth and sterueth [dies],
> That out of couent and cloistre coueyteth to dwelle.
> For yf heuene be on thys erthe other eny eyse for saule,
> Hit is in cloistre other in scole by meny skyles ich fynde.
> For in cloistre cometh no man to chide ne to fighte;
> In scole ys loue and lownesse and lykyng to lerne.
> Ac [but] meny day, men telleth bothe monkes and
>   chanouns
> Han ride out of a-ray [proper place] here ruele vuel
>   [evil] yholde [consider],
> Lederes [leaders] of louedaies [law days (often ex-
>   ploited)] and landes purchassed,
> And priked a-boute on palfrais fro places [mansions] to
>   maners,
> An hepe of houndes at hus ers as he a lord were;
> And but [unless] hus knaue knele that shal hus coppe
>   holde,
> He loketh al louryng and 'lordein' [lazy rascal] hym
>   calleth."   (C VI, 147–63)

Reason, who utters these lines as part of a sermon, can hold an
ideal as an absolute. In a church-oriented society it *should* be true
that the nearest thing to heaven is life within convent and cloister.

For the Dreamer, however, the matter is otherwise: both outside *and* inside the convent the nuns are, in his church-weary eyes,
no better than the monks. First, discoursing with Reason, the
Dreamer says, ". . . monkes and moniales [nuns] that mendi-
nauns sholden fynde [provide for], / Han made here [their] kyn
knyghtes and knyghtfees [incomes] purchased" (C VI, 76–77). As
though admitting that he himself is guilty of waxing choleric on
the subject, Langland puts in the mouth of Wrath a later speech
on the subject of cloistered nuns, and we should note the contrast
with Reason's remarks on chiding and fighting. Wrath says:

"Ich haue be cook in here kychene and the couent serued
Meny monthes with hem and with monkes bothe.
Ich was the prioresse potager and other poure ladies,
And made here ioutes [pottages] of iangles [quarrels]; 'dame
    Iohane was a bastarde,
And dame Clarice a knyghtes douhter a cokewold [cuckold]
    was hure syre,
Dame Purnele a prestes file prioresse worth [will become]
    hue neuere;
For hue hadde a childe in the chapon-cote [hen-house] hue
    worth [was] chalenged at eleccion.'
Thus thei sitte, tho [those] sustres som tyme, and disputen,
Til 'thow lixt [lie]' and 'thow lixt' be lady ouer hem alle;"
                              (C VII, 130–38)

At a great distance from the simple and contemplative peace of
cloistered life are the parish priests and parsons who complain
that their parishes are poor and seek permission to dwell in London "And synge ther for symonye for seluer ys swete" (C I, 84).
Parsons, says Reason, have no pity for the poor (C VI, 167).
There are those who take advantage of city life as a regular thing:
"Bisshopes and bachilers [novices] bothe maisters and doctors . . . / Thei lyen in Londone in lentene, and elles. / Somme
seruen the kynge and hus seluer tellen [count]" (C I, 85–90).
Skeat explains the overlapping here of ecclesiastical and legal
roles, with the clerics making inroads on the lawyer's rightful pre-
cincts. These interlopers in exchequer and chancery are accused
by Conscience of encouraging idolatry.

The Lady Holychurch has a kind word for chaplains. Many,
she observes, are chaste (C II, 187); but, she goes on to say, charity fails them. She continues in rather ordinary language to indict
their avarice, unkindness to their kin and to all Christians. Her
last thought turns from the clergy to "alle cristine" and to love as
the way to heaven. Also raked in passing in various parts of the
poem are rectors, archdeacons, and beadsmen.

II *Higher Offices*

Not even a bishop's high office is protection from Langland's
wrath. Conscience, describing parsons and priests, hints by association that bishops are not only "lewd" but worse:

"Hue [Mede] blesseth thees byshopys thauh [though]
    thei be negh lewede,
Hue prouendreth persons prestes hue menteyneth
To holde lemmanes and lotebyes [concubines] al here
    lif-dayes,
And bryngeth forth barnes a-ȝens for-boden lawes;"
                                        (C IV, 186–89)

Reason adds his clear voice in scoring these episcopal wrong-
doers. In his opinion, bishops' horses, hawks, and hounds should
be sold and the money spent on housing for beggars or to help
"poor religious" (B IV, 124–26). In a speech of two hundred eighty-
eight lines which straddles two passus in C (the speaker is not
identified in B), Recklessness "a-resonede" (argued with) "cler-
gie." In B, the unidentified speaker says "I haue wonder for why
and wher-fore the bisshop / Maketh suche prestes that lewed men
bytrayen" (B XI, 294–95). In C, Recklessness expands on their
remissness: "Vuele [evil] ben thei suffred [allowed] suche that
schenden [spoil] masses / Throgh hure luther [wicked] lyuynge
and lewede vnder-stondyng!" (C XIV, 115–16). Recklessness then
turns from careless scribes to careless priests: "So is he a goky
[fool], by god that in the godspel failleth, / In masse other in
matynes maketh eny defaute" (121–22).

The ultimate responsibility is the bishop's (or the Pope's):

"The bishop shal be blamed by-fore god, as ich leyue
    [believe],
That coroneth [tonsures] suche clerkes as for godes
    knyghtes [servants],
That conneth [know] nat *sapienter* nother [neither]
    synge ne rede.
Ac neyther is al blameles the bisshop ne the chapeleyn;
For *ignorantia non excusat* as ich haue herd in bookes."
                                        (124–28)

(In the same vein, Conscience had earlier rebuked bishops for
encouraging parsons and priests to serve Lady Meed.)

The Pope is drawn into the gamut as Lady Meed explains that
"The pope and alle prelates presentes vnder-fongen [accept] /
And ȝeuen mede to men to menteynye here lawes." (C IV,
272–73). But the Dreamer himself, in a dialogue with Reason, ven-

tures the strongest comment on popes in general: "Popes and pa-
trones poure [poor] gentil blod refuseth, / And taken Symondes
[simony's] sone seyntewarie [sanctuary] to kepe" (C VI, 78–79).

With the popes our catalogue of wayward clergy is complete in
its range of least to greatest, if not comprehensive of all types.
Langland's care in singling out so many separate ranks and orders
is undoubtedly due to his wish that no one of the culpable should
escape the pointing finger.

Despite all this satirical breadth, the final remark to be made on
the subject of anticlericalism must needs be a positive one. There
is no blanket condemnation of the clergy. On the contrary, Langland speaks idealistically of the proper functions of worthy members. The character Clergy himself, if not a hero, is yet no villain.
Everyone uses meed: there is no choice in an economy which is,
in a manner of speaking, on the gold standard. But Langland
charges the clergy with far more than commercialism. What he is
saying is that a clergy is necessary but that failures and defections
are abundant and that each pardoner, summoner, friar, and priest
must improve his professional conduct.

III   *The Trades*

Langland's practice of specific address in making accusations
carries over into portions of the narrative in which the laity have
particular involvement. Again, individual trades and professions,
like the orders and ranks of clergy, are shown to be corrupt and
are presented in sufficient variety so that practically everyone
above the status of common laborer is touched. As with the clergy,
Langland begins to focus his attack early in the poem. In C I, 224,
the clause "that don here dedes ille" by its position directly modifies "dikers [ditchers] and deluers." But the series of compound
nouns, tightened by the parallel *as* phrases, creates an ambiguity.
Does the *that* clause modify only "dikers and deluers," or shall it
be taken as a description of all the tradesmen and laborers mentioned in the sentence?

> Al ich sauh slepyng as ʒe shullen hure after;
> Bothe bakers and brywers bouchers and othere,
> Webbesters [female weavers] and walkers [fullers]
>   and wynners with handen,
> As taylours and tanners and tyliers of erthe,

As dikers and deluers that don here dedes ille,
And dryueth forth hure daies with *"deux saue
dame Emme!"* [2]   (C I, 220–25)

Surely ditchers and diggers were not the only singers of frivolous
songs. As for dishonest practice, brewers (most of them women,
as Skeat reminds us [C VII, 226]) were among the more notorious cheats.[3] Spicers are likewise guilty. We remember that Glutton, when he was offered a drink on his way to church, asked if
they had any spices. Like beer and pretzels of a later time, ale and
spices were natural complements; and, as in any century, purvey-
ors of drink and the food that goes with it were often on the far
edge of the law. Spicers, says Langland, are in league with Liar
himself (C III, 235–36).

Of drapiers, Langland says that they stretch the cloth when
they measure it to sell and that clothiers comb wool with avarice
"to deceyue the puple" (XII, 15–16). Weavers use an overweight
pound on the scales (VII, 221–24). In general, however, small
tradesmen and laborers, as members of the working class, are represented as the virtuous victims of the more wealthy and power-
ful. Mayors, officers of the courts, sheriffs "punyshen on pillories
and on pynyng [paining]-stoles, / . . . bakers and brewers
bouchers and cokes" (C IV, 77–80).

Langland is not grieving over troubles besetting the high and
the mighty. His concern is for the little people, mistreated by their
betters but chosen by Christ as His own. Their poverty is a condition necessary for salvation: long, hard hours of work keep one
out of mischief. There is never an ill word for *hewes* (workmen);
indeed, they are praised many times over. None, Langland says,
are sooner saved or firmer in their faith than plowmen and the
poor common people (C XII, 292–93).

IV *Secular Professions*

And so, as in the large part of satirical writing, it is the rich
merchants, the doctors, the fashionable minstrels and jugglers and
all their ilk who are specifically attacked, like the clergy. Langland is particularly harsh in speaking of medical doctors. After the
pardoners had sheltered Liar and restored his strength, "Thanne
lourede [scowled] leches and letters thei senten / That Lyer shold

wony [dwell] with hem waters [urine of patients] to loke [observe]" (C III, 233–34). Doctors and jugglers are treated similarly in being grouped with whores and bawds. Of doctors Conscience says bluntly, "Harlotes and hores and al-so false leches, / Thei asken hure huyre [hire] er [before] they hit haue deserued" (C IV, 302–3). Of the jugglers Piers says:

> "Ich shal fynde hem fode that feythfullech lybben;
> Saf Iack the iogelour and Ionette of the styues [stews],
> And Danyel the dees-pleyere and Denote the baude,"
> (C IX, 70–72)

Besides collecting fees before they are earned, doctors are guilty of another kind of prematureness, and let there be no mistake, says Hunger, about the percentage of malpractitioners: "Ther aren meny luthere [wicked] leches and leele [honest] leches fewe, / Thei don [cause] men deye thorgh here drynkes er [before] destyne hit wolde [wished]" (C IX, 296–97). Since the profession was not at that time divided in the slivers of specialization, Langland treats it as all of a piece.

Another profession is law, toward which Langland has a different attitude—neutrality. Law the abstraction is an absolute in his mind as he presents it in both ecclesiastical and civil form, and he speaks of it throughout the poem as an ideal toward which men must aspire.[4] In one passage there is reprobation of "men that kepen lawes," but the phrase is not exclusive and may identify various types of civil servants. In C it is replaced by the phrase "othere stywardes," perhaps because of Langland's reluctance to include lawyers in his satire.

> Salamon the sage a sarmoun he made,
> For to amende maires and men that kepen lawes,
> And tolde hem this teme [text] that I telle thynke;
> *Ignis deuorabit tabernacula eorum qui libenter
> accipiunt munera, etc.*
> Amonge this lettered ledes [people] this latyn is to
> mene,
> That fyre shal falle, and brenne [burn] al to blo
> [pale] askes
> The houses and the homes of hem that desireth
> ȝiftes or ȝeresȝyues [New Year's gifts] bi-cause of
> here offices.   (B III, 93–99)

For Langland there was little if any distinction between divine and human law. When he speaks of transgressors against "the law," he often mixes sinners and criminals—lechers, thieves, cattle traders—thus revealing his view of law as a unity. Often as the clergy are taken to task, their ministering of justice is not criticized. Langland was well aware of the differences in jurisdiction and procedure of ecclesiastical and civil courts and also aware that these were not truly distinct from each other at any time in the Middle Ages and that bishops and monks often pre-empted full civil authority in what were for all purposes civil courts. The clergy's assumption of civil authority, while itself an extra-legal circumstance, was a very old story, something to be taken for granted, and Langland shows no concern. As we have seen, he finds the clergy reprehensible in their failure to fulfill their vows of poverty, chastity, and obedience—not in their adjudicating functions in their own courts or in their meddling with the courts of the state.

He had much knowledge of the legal profession, whose members' firsthand, red-handed experience of the Seven Deadly Sins, we may assume, was equal to that of the rest of the folk in the fair field. Perhaps the implication is that the sacredness of the law is not affected by the private lives of its custodians. This speculation may be quite wrong, and the hard-to-get-at truth may be (but how improbable it is) that instead of any such notion, Langland felt so much partiality for lawyers that he exempted them or (even more unlike his character) that he was fearful of incurring the enmity of the courts.

As in his generalizations about the other professions and occupations, Langland is benevolent toward minstrelsy, acknowledging this main source of public pleasure. He sees minstrels, nevertheless, as people whose lives lack rigor and discipline, who live too easily and voluptuously. In one of the passages which fall most strangely on modern ears, professional minstrels are differentiated from "mynstrales of heuene." These latter, we are shocked to learn, are the lunatics and lepers whose ravings amuse normal folk. There is no derision in this attitude, of course: mental defectives in particular were fed and protected as having been touched by God. No doubt the reputations of God-obsessed ascetics had helped these unfortunates to win their special status.

Langland's own sympathy and respect for "lunatik lollers and leperes" is clearly heard:

> . . . hem wanteth here witt men and women bothe,
> The whiche aren lunatik lollers and leperes a-boute,
> And mad as the moone sitt [sits] more other lasse.
> Thei caren for no cold ne counteth of no hete,
> And arn meuynge [moving] after [according to] the
>   mone moneyles thei walke,
> With a good wil, witlees meny wyde contreys,
> Ryght as Peter dude [did] and Paul saue that thei preche
>   nat,
> Ne myracles maken . . .
> Hit [they] arn as hus aposteles, suche puple other as his
>   priuye disciples.
> For he [God] sente hem forth seluerles in a somer garne-
>   ment,
> With-oute bred and bagge as the bok telleth . . .
> Barfot and bredles beggeth thei of no man.
> And thauh he mete with the meyre [mayor] amyddes
>   the strete,
> He [lunatic] reuerenceth hym ryght nouht no rather
>   [more readily] than another . . .
> Suche manere of men Matheu ous techeth,
> We sholde haue hem to house and help hem when thei
>   come . . .
> For hit aren murye-mouthede men mynstrales of heuene,
> And godes boyes [followers], bordiours [jesters] . . .
>   (C X, 106–27)[5]

This passage is an example of Langland's ability to combine a number of ingredients that please the modern reader. The phrasing, if not the idea, of "mad as the moone sitt," followed by the flippant "more other lasse," makes a striking line. Unsentimental compassion for the witless wanderers sounds the right note. Humor insinuates again as the mayor goes unsaluted, and the epithets at the end poke gentle irony and elevate the idiots to celestial choirs at the same time. The thought in this passage is a repetition of a statement which is more specific but less intriguing in form:

Clerkus and knyȝtes welcometh kynges mynstrales,
And for loue of here lordes lithen [listen to] hem at festes;
Muche more, me thenketh riche men auhte
Haue beggers by-fore hem whiche beth godes mynstrales,
(C VIII, 97–100)

It is plain that the minstrels whom Langland complains about are
the worldly professionals. In C IV, 277, they ask for meed. They
are like friars and doctors in harboring Liar for months at a time
(C III, 237–38).

Langland's severest castigation of minstrels is heard in the
opening lines of the poem, when human types are slashed bare to
their imperfections. He is telling of minstrels

That wollen neyther swynke [work] ne swete bote swery
    grete othes,
And fynde vp foule fantesyes and foles hem [of themselves]
    maken,
And hauen witte at wylle to worche yf they wolde.
(C I, 36–38)

Since they have "wit at will," these obviously are not the "God's
minstrels" mentioned in the later passus. Langland's position here
is a familiar one. He recognizes the usefulness of minstrels—undoubtedly heard them with an enjoyment beyond the capacity of
ordinary laymen. Nevertheless, generalizing as always, making no
distinction between diligent genius and indolent droners of borrowed songs, he insists that they all need drastically to improve.

In his many explorations of beggars' lanes and princely courts,
of stews and monasteries, Langland comes again and again to two
vices: avarice (and sometimes to related gluttony, more rarely to
lechery—also related); and sloth. Although pride has classical priority in church catalogues of the seven—and in epic and in romance—this sin is seldom named directly by Langland. But, if we
harken to his incessant pleading for the poor and to his exaltation
of the humble station in this life, there is no doubt that he accepts
the common view of pride as the central sin, the original sin and
the ultimate, the weakness that seems strength in the city of man.
Pride is not specified because it is everywhere to be found, the
mastering sin that saturates *Piers Plowman*.

V *Salvation*

Langland's audience were undoubtedly grateful for the new fare which he spread before them. But they could hardly feel flattered, for his poem is a satire whose target is the human race; and, taken to heart, its comments on human frailty are sobering for all and probably depressing for the more guilty among us. Typically nonconformist, in his capacity as satirist Langland does something different from the usual treatment of Fallen Man. Whereas most satirists engagingly point out with wagging finger that we are clay at bottom and leave us feeling naughty or vaguely guilty at worst—but mightily amused—the lone master from the Midlands writes with another aim.

He takes the conventional stance and catalogues man's wickedness; but beyond that he actually hopes, unlike practically all of the other great satirists, to make an improvement. No Utopian, he has no thought of undoing the apple-in-Eden by molding living saints out of sinners. Sin will infest the earth until the last day; and the question is, therefore, what is going to happen after that. Here, to restress the idea which I and many before me have harped upon, Langland is at the core of his purpose. Salvation, in spite of the ubiquitous occasions of sin and the unavoidable weakenings, is all his thought. This objective being true, it can also be said that no satirist of Langland's acid strength ever wrote with his ambidexterity. He tells us with piercing words how bad we are. In a changing mood he bends our gaze upward; over the tops of the dunghill castles and their burning banners he makes us strain toward an eternity of new life. He also hopes that perfection in earthly life can be attained in the process, but I believe he recognized the ordinary man's incapacity.

CHAPTER 6

Puns and Pairs in Glad Procession

AFTER Chaucer's works, the Middle English poem most extensively discussed has been *Piers Plowman*. The authorship controversy produced a sizable body of critical writings; and interpretations of the poem's didactic content, both religious and sociological, have been so systematic and so numerous that our understanding of the entire area of late medieval literature has been enriched. Yet, despite this vast collective effort, one aspect of the poem has, until recently, gone virtually unremarked. With a few exceptions, the standard practice has been for critics to mention Langland's puns on his own name and beyond these to ignore the element of word-play altogether. So preoccupied have they been with what seemed at the time more important considerations that even the lines which they have quoted in isolation have gone through their nervous systems with never a prickle, although many of these lines contain word-play of one type or another.

Moreover, word-play often provides clues to Langland's motive in altering a given line. The C text, for example, lags far behind the two earlier texts in number and quality of word-plays illustrated by my tabulations below, where each line or phrase quoted was chosen for its superiority over the versions of the word-play, if any, in the other two texts. Various attempts to explain the relative flatness of the C text which have not taken into account puns and similar devices have resulted in statements like Manly's: "There are [in the C text] multitudinous alterations of single words or phrases, sometimes to secure better alliteration, sometimes to get rid of an archaic word, sometimes to modify an opinion, but often for no discoverable reason. . . ." [1] E. T. Donaldson calls the line "And sawe meny cellis [cells] and selcouthe [strange] thynges" (C I, 5) "poetically dubious," apparently disregarding the play on *cel-sel*.[2] Similarly passed over are ". . . ratones [rats] at ones" (B Pr. 145), and ". . . Belial thy belsyre

. . ." (C XXI, 284). In her chapter on Wulfstan's canon, Dorothy Bethurum cites several pairs of words, some of which—"mærð [glory] 7 myrhð [mirth]," "forloren 7 forlogen"—might be further classified as specimens of *annominatio*.[3]

The best discussion of Middle English puns to date is that of Bernard F. Huppé.[4] I can add very little to Huppé's illumination of the variety and subtleties of Langland's word-play and the cohesive function of puns, homonyms, and redundancies, which Huppé examines in the light of pure rhetoric. To the rhetorician, "serious" word-play, as Huppé describes Langland's, is a fundamental and familiar part of medieval religious writing. I have no quarrel with this view, and I am sure that Langland would welcome each stratifying probe of his lines.

In the course of his treatment of Langland's rhetorical devices, Huppé, reaching far down to the lowest order of pun, the type traditionally entitled *annominatio* (*adnominatio*), explains the function of the puns as integral parts of the structure of *Piers Plowman*. It is on this lower level that I shall supplement his work; and, to do so, two types of word-play will be represented, the second of which (herein to be called the "matched pair") is even less exalted than *annominatio*. Around this latter term revolve definitions which differ remarkably from each other.

For the present, the term should be understood as designating a pun involving two or more words which are distinct from each other in meaning but which the manuscripts spell either identically or with very slight difference—usually the difference of one letter. Almost all of the punning syllables, which are not necessarily the initial syllables, can be said to be alliterative. Many of the examples of puns brought forth in this study probably do not fit the popular conception of the pun as a single word with double meaning. *Annominatio* is by far Langland's favorite type of pun and is one of his three favorite structural devices. (There are four, if alliteration and the four-stress pattern are taken separately.) Another device, the matched pair, is defined and illustrated below.

At its best—that is, in its most successful combinations—*annominatio* in Piers Plowman functions in the following manner. When the two (or sometimes three or four) words of different denotation are brought shoulder to shoulder or, in some cases, within a line of each other, there is a transfer of second meaning to one of them, and even reciprocally to both in a few instances. The word which has gained new meaning retains its etymologically "true" meaning, but supplements the matched word, its source of "second" meaning, by obliquely conveying a notion of, for example: weariness, ". . . wery of that werke . . ." (B XV, 181); grief, ". . . grete [weep] and gret doel . . ." (B V, 386); suffering, ". . . tene [vex] no tenaunt . . ." (B VI, 39). These three are obvious, while others are obscure. Some are funny; many, to be sure, are "bad"; all, I believe, are interesting, even when removed from context.[5]

Discounting all repetition of puns in parallel passages, there are over five hundred puns (the term will be understood to translate *annominatio* throughout the remainder of this chapter) in *Piers Plowman*. This is a staggering total; but, when the length of the poem is considered, the puns, which are seen below to be fairly evenly distributed, cannot be said to weave the poem line by line into a unit. They help in its unification, and they keep us reminded of Langland's humanness. An estimate of their effect should not be made, however, until another, related device is taken into account.

Whereas the importance of the pun in *Piers Plowman* was long ago at least guessed at by Skeat and more recently described with great thoroughness by Huppé, Langland's second device, which shall for want of a better name and because of syntactic parallelism be called the matched pair (see p. 105), has received no notice in any printed commentary on *Piers Plowman* known to me. Dorothy Bethurum speaks of "parallelism of word and clause" in the homilies of Wulfstan.[6] Continuing, she says,

The linking of two nouns, often synonyms, often alliterating, occurs very frequently, as *maerð 7 myrhð, sorgung 7 sargung, wealdend 7 wyrhta*. The habit of duplication applies to other parts of speech also, and became fixed in Wulfstan's mature writing, as in *magan 7 motan, oft 7 gelome, swutol 7 gesene, þafode 7 þolode*. Alliteration is a constant feature of his homilies, sometimes used in a single instance, sometimes through a long paragraph of heightened writing; sometimes with an obvious hammering effect, sometimes unobtrusively. What has been less often commented on is the frequency of rhyme, both in rhymed combinations paralleling the alliterative ones, such as *aelc broc 7 nan bot, hine man band 7 hine man swang, forloren 7 forlogen,* and in the less formal way in which alliteration is used, as in the English part of Homily XIX.[7]

Professor Bethurum obviously regards the *annominatio* and the matched pair as being very closely related, as indeed they are; but she passes over "forloren [lost] 7 forlogen [lied]" (above) in finding examples of two-word puns. She states that in addition to the features described in the quotation above,

Wulfstan was fond of a sort of play on words in which he uses two compound words with the same root but different meanings, something approaching a pun, as in *man byð þonne beswicen 7 deofol ah ða saule butan he geswice* (VI. 89–90); *forbugan aelc unrihte 7 gebugan georne to rihte* (XIII. 54–55); *Godes gerihta mid rihte gelaeste* (XX. 27); *fela ungelimpa gelimð* (XX. 108). Some of the best effects come from this play on words, at which Wulfstan became more and more adept as he gained in experience.[8]

The last sentence could be applied to Langland; also the following from the section on Wulfstan's style (this sentence is immediately preceded by a reference to word-play in *Piers Plowman*): "Often he [Wulfstan] uses it [word-play] to give a shock of surprise, though, fond as he was of puns, he did not use them for purely humorous effects."[9] The resemblance between word-play in Langland, who was a homilist in spirit and in certain technical respects, and the word-play in Wulfstan is not pointed out, though it might be.[10]

It is reassuring to read someone who speaks of a medieval writer as being "fond . . . of puns" and of the "humorous effects" of puns. My own chief purpose in analyzing Langland's word-play is to show the lighter side of Langland, who goes much beyond the Pearl Poet and incomparably farther than Chaucer in punning and who often reveals a playful impulse to enliven the weightiest passus with a peppering of puns and other lexical sparks whose main justifications are word-fun and harmony of sounds. To be sure, Langland uses word-play in conformance with the manuals of rhetoric, but he may not have used the manuals to any great extent.[11]

Perhaps the many who have visualized him as a stern and somber personality were somewhat justified by the serious and didactic nature of most of his work and by the common associations of melancholy with a lean and lanky physique. But there is another Langland, and a complete portrait requires that we take into account all of the qualities of his writing, including his brilliant strokes of description, scenes of dramatic excitement, high comedy, earthy and sometimes bawdy vocabulary—also, perhaps as significant as any of these, the fiber and texture of lines that are woven with word-play.

The opinion which sees only turgid allegory and vague, outdated popular theology is also obviously unfair. Most unfortunate is the attitude commonly taken by students enrolled in medieval and survey courses who dismiss the poem without reading it, even in a translation. They read *about* it, and their instructor repeatedly mentions it in passing; but it is a rare class which actually swoops down and settles on the poem for any length of time. With every right to do so, modern taste favors the short stories of Chaucer and the romance and the ballad, but high priorities need not be exclusive choices. And, if the teachers themselves would do *Piers Plowman* the honor of a careful reading first, then kindle the interest of their classes—and this should not be hard—a great work that has been generally untouched would attain at least the level of recognition now held by the *Faerie Queene,* the postmedieval masterwork which has been most neglected and, by some, abused.

Considering the esteem which word-play has always enjoyed and considering that on the average at least a few specimens of word-play are present on each page of *Piers Plowman,* as readers we should be enticed to keep turning the pages of *Piers Plowman,* even if we are on the trail of word-play and nothing else. Strongest enticement will emanate from the puns, for they are at once more obscure and more rewarding when digging brings them into the light. Their only inferiority to the matched pairs is of a phonological nature; the pairs indisputably are more musical—in fact, often exist for little else than musical effect.

I   Annominatio

The puns in the lists that follow cover a wide range of relative quality, and many of the least effective and the downright pointless are mere accidents unnoticed by Langland; or, if noticed by him, they seemed to be of as little importance as they do to us today. At the other extreme are examples of *annominatio* at its versatile best—two flints striking sparks whenever they touch in the reader's mind, and doing it melodiously. Instead of making a display of my personal favorites at this point, I leave the selective columns in the Appendix (p. 129) to the reader's own discoveries. His reactions will be unique, since they will be filtered through his own peculiar intensional equipment and even some extensional variations, as well as his experience with Middle English poetry, and then we must add Old English, and not forget that people's reactions to any and all puns differ remarkably. Surely there is a feast here for everyone with a taste for puns.

Two hundred sixty-one puns of special note are given in the Appendix. Each excerpt is taken from the text (A, B, or C) in which the punning word or words are most suitably spelled. I have not recorded repetition of a pun in parallel passages of one or both of the other texts: the references in parentheses are to repetitions *below* the line quoted. The pages of quoted lines are followed by tabulations of approximately four hundred line numbers of the more ordinary and predictable variety often repeated in *Piers Plowman* and other alliterative poems.

II *Alliterating Matched Pairs*

Everyone who has read *Piers Plowman* has witnessed the steady procession of matched pairs across its pages. What had not been noticed, it seems, is the application which Langland made of matched pairs in his design for the structure of *Piers Plowman*. If redundant and nonredundant are counted together, the total number of these alliterating doublets is over one thousand! Appearing in such numbers and with such regularity and being so closely akin to the puns, they may be said to complete the particular kind of subthematic continuity begun by the puns. If, before the matched pairs took our notice, we felt that word-play had a cohesive effect on parts of the poem, but not on the whole, we now, viewing puns and matched pairs together, perceive in them components which bind the whole poem.

Annominatio and matched pair make a good working team. *Annominatio* lends rhetorical point to the pair; in fact, because of their frequency, the puns can be said to induce in the reader a habit of making close association between similar words. The result is that, though the members of a matched pair lack the morphologic resemblance necessary to a pun, they still participate in a kind of mutual semantic assimilation. Darkness is dreadful, and dread is dark in "derkenesse and drede" (B XVI, 85). To the medieval mind, the adjectives in "syke and synful" (B XVI, 109) would have inevitable associations. "For mede ne for mone" emphasizes the usual basis for earthly meed. Priority is emphasized in "formest and ferst" (C VII, 15).[12] Other types of pairs are briefly discussed at the end of this section.

Just as the matched pairs gain something by being in the company of *annominatio,* the puns are also reinforced by the presence of their lowly relatives, the pairs. The most prolific of punning authors suffer certain inescapable limitations: opportunities for good puns are never omnipresent, no matter what the context may be; decorum of a kind usually ignored by James Joyce restrains most writers, and enough of a good thing is simply enough; not all intended puns will be apprehended by the audience (how many we miss in Chaucer and in Langland is anybody's guess). Langland's puns are, thus, not few; but it is sometimes far between them. Yet it would seem farther if it were not for the ubiquitous matched pairs. The effect is something like that of a necklace strung with pearls and crystals.

Second only to *annominatio* in importance as word-play, the matched pair consists of two or three alliterating words which are syntactically alike in their sentence. All of the alliterating pairs tabulated in the Appendix are syntactically matched and may best be called "matched pairs." The frequency of them in *Piers Plowman* is twice that of the puns. Over twenty-five per cent are redundant. All of them help to invest the poem with a strong verbal spice. Or, to approach them from another point of view, they could be called glances from writer to reader which suggest that to be sure the matter of the poem is serious, but we need not become desperate over it. As Langland uses them, they are, like the puns, a symptom of the irrepressible joy of living which offset the medieval Christian's skeptical outlook on the city of man.

In large measure, then, the pairs provide relief from Langland's sober preachments. Within the line, the pair charges itself by setting up associations between the two, or occasionally three, words involved. It has, thus, some of the transfer of meaning which has already been observed as happening in the punning lines. Indeed, the two devices are not absolutely distinct from each other. The puns, let us say, are more pungent. Because the components of the matched pair usually have only the alliterating initial sounds in common, the effects, humorous and otherwise, are considerably less than those of the puns. Nevertheless, the pairs reinforce many a line in a variety of ways—by accretion of denotations (". . . with swynke and with swot . . ." [C IX, 241]); by blunt-pointed antitheses, most of which are fixed phrases (". . . thi frende and thi foo . . ." [B IX, 200]); by redundancies (". . . harlotes and hores . . ." [B XV, 130]); and by simple repetitions.

Within the portion of a line which contains a matched pair, a distinctive rhythm prevails—either a one-syllable word before the conjunctive *and* followed by a word of two or more syllables, or words of equal number of syllables both before and after the conjunctive *and*. Exceptions, such as "With bakbitynge and bismer" (B V, 89), are so few as to be negligible. In "Withoute lycence and leue" (C VII, 121), what we actually have is a pair of two-syllable nouns. Although all but a fraction of the pairs lie in the first hemistich, before caesura, the presence of an adjunct phrase (even after caesura) which modifies only one of the seemingly paired words prevents, to my ear, the formation of a perfect pair. For example, in "Thanne ich crie and cracche with my kene nailes" (C VII, 140), the prepositional phrase modifying *cracche* spoils the balance necessary to a matched pair.

Occasionally caesura separates a matched pair from a third member which has no modifying phrase and which does not couple with a word in its own, the second, hemistich ("We sholde be lowe and loueliche and leel, eche man to other" [C XIII, 129]). Since *leel* may be read with secondary or even tertiary stress, this line may be said to contain the pair "lowe and loueliche," and not a three-adjective set. Most of the third matching words have been, I believe, partitioned off from the matched pair by the poet, who apparently designed the entire work with the idea of placing his matched pairs in the first hemistich, undoubtedly the best position for telling effect. For another example, "With techinge or with tilynge or trauaylynge of hondes" (A VII, 235) does not qualify with a three-word set for three reasons: the third *with* is lacking; *trauaylynge,* the third noun, is followed by the phrase *of hondes;* normally, the third member has the same number of syllables as the other two members.

Not easily to be explained are variations in the frequency of
matched pairs, which make original appearances in largest number in A, in B XI–XX, and in C XII–XXI. Perhaps before he wrote
a word of *Piers Plowman,* Langland had resolved to put the
matched pair to heavy use and did not waste a page in getting
on with his plan. Puns, on the other hand, accumulate slowly in
the early stage of the poem. Then there is a quickening, as though
the poet, after paying almost exclusive attention to matched pairs
from the outset, now realizes that there is a rich potential in
annominatio. Although the pairs increase only moderately from
C XII onward, through XXI, that is, *annominatio* continues
strongly, and along with it certain intensives—particularly *al*—
are used more frequently than before. Since, like the intensives,
pairs and puns often lend force and emphasis, these effects may
perhaps be called emotional indicators during the period of
Langland's production of the latter half of the final version, as,
for example, in B XV.[13]

When he was revising (B I–X, C I–XXIII) he was slightly more
assiduous, in general, in finding new pairs for C than for B, with
the one conspicuous exception of the opening pages of the poem.
This comparison is not perfectly equable, of course, since C,
having retained most of the pairs which appear in B, attracts
extra credit for the strenuous task of adding to their bulk. It was
more difficult for C to build on B (and therefore indirectly on
A) than for B to build on A.

There is a temptation to speculate further—to shrink the gaps
in time between the versions and to show Langland as being still
much occupied with the pairs in writing the entire B version, then
his interest tapering off and not rising again to a steady high level
until he was well into C. B would then have been begun soon
after A was finished, and indeed the matched pair is applied with
greater frequency in B XI–XX than anywhere else and on the
smallest scale in C I–X.

Context is also a factor; B C I and II and C III are relatively
quiet and mostly narrative but not highly dramatic. And so these
passus, as well as A I and II, are rather light in the number of
matched pairs. High rhetoric, lyricism, turbulence are lacking.

But to us hunters of the man behind the poem it is the general
change, the rising frequency of pairs in B and C, which is most

important. For this infusion invites the plausible interpretation that Langland's liking for pairs grew side by side with his control of them. If he indulged himself, he was not indecorous, since the result of the additions is ornamentation and greater force. And yet there is a suggestion of sentiment in one who to such an extent—almost an extreme—exploits a device whose effects are often sentimental. In short, if we had not other evidence of his sympathies and emotions, the writer's extravagance in this regard would make an impression of a certain warmth and sensitivity.

The foregoing guesses, which are no better than guesses, could be blown away by the likely but not testable element of accident. Possibly the waxing and waning of Langland's enthusiasm for matched pairs is to be explained by the influence of his reading at a given time, the state of his happiness, the matter of context referred to above.

III   *The Rhetoric of* Piers Plowman *and Old English Homilies*

While it is true that, as a general thing, all alliterative Old and Middle English writing contains matched pairs, it is also obvious that there is not space here to discuss the rhetorical relationships between *Piers Plowman* and all of that vast body of literature. Long aware of this type of relationship where Old English homilies are concerned, I was prompted by the comments of Bethurum and Funke to go to the earliest extant English homiletic writings. From these I have chosen a group of Anglo-Saxon homilists, mostly anonymous, of the tenth and eleventh centuries as representing an earlier tradition in the use of *annominatio* and matched pair; and I have compared this usage in the Old and Middle English works.[14] Word-play, as I shall show, is of shifting importance in Old English homilies, depending upon the homilist; but it is present in all homiliaries to some extent. My point is, then, that *Piers Plowman* and the homilies have, in addition to the parallels on which G. R. Owst has elaborated,[15] one distinctive rhetorical feature concerning which the critics of the poem and the critics of the homilies have been almost silent.

The homiliaries involved are earlier than the sermons of Bromyard, Brinton, and Rypon to which Owst makes the largest part of his references. (In Owst's two books, Aelfric, Wulfstan, the Blickling homilies are barely mentioned; the Vercelli, not at all. Other anonymous homilies from which I shall draw are also not mentioned by Owst.) *Piers Plowman*, on the other hand, is the poem which most often is brought into his discussions of satire and complaint. It would result in much repetition if his compilations of analogues between *Piers Plowman* and homilies dated post-1100 were extended so that the pre-1100 homilies were accounted for. What Owst says about the later homilies applies as well to the earlier ones if these are viewed in a general way as a homogeneous group. Another reason for resting content with his exegetical analysis of ideas, archetypal characters, and other literary and homiletic conventions in *Piers Plowman* is simply that the earlier homilies to a large extent consist of one kind of religious material of which Langland makes only incidental use: the lives of the saints. He does little more, in fact, than to name the Church Fathers and the Evangelists and a sprinkling of other saints for a total of twenty-five.

Why did the preacher Langland forego the natural medium of the sermon? For centuries the best of pulpit oratory had been tethered on a level where novelty was rare and formal convention as highly prized as it was to be later in the English Augustan period. The greatest of all medieval English preachers, Aelfric of Eynsham, wrote both in prose and verse; and the latter was cast in the long alliterative line, though not consistently. As prose stylist, he is rightly crowned "the outstanding scholar and prose stylist of the late Old English period" [16] and one who had "genius as a teacher." [17] His alliterative lives of the saints are less pointedly didactic than his homilies, being generally eventful rather than expository or exhortatory. In this respect, they resemble *Piers Plowman;* but, except for alliteration, there is almost nothing in common structurally. The *Lives* are in fact so inconsistent in both meter and alliteration that there will always be a doubt as to the most suitable typography—plain prose, as with the *Catholic Homilies*, or the four-beat line with caesura. As Skeat sets up the *Lives*, some lines are marked for caesura; some are not. The organization of all of Aelfric's homilies, including the saints' lives, has the simplicity of the church calendar. In contrast, the complicating joints of Langland's poem grate each other in tension.

Individual homilies, by Aelfric or any others of the Old English period, are also, with few exceptions, simply constructed and have the principal aim of teaching and edification. Entertainment is a consideration, but only a minor one; *Piers Plowman,* on the other hand, is designed for entertainment, as I argue throughout much of this book. I do not mean to suggest that the great homilists had esthetic myopia or that Langland was a tireless *jongleur* who never descended from the summit of art. The homilists too were creative, and, in spite of the confinements of their medium, they often acquitted themselves as artists. I do believe, however, that whether or not he was always conscious of it, Langland sought the pleasure of his reader more diligently than did any other of the medieval English writers of sermon, satire, and complaint. Proof lies in the grandeur of vision, the beauty of diction and imagery, the music that strains his control, and the puns and pairs, and the motley characters. He has dull moments—for us more of them than there were for the readers in or near his own time. But again —compared with the sameness of tone, vocabulary, and themes of the homilies—his poem is swift, startling, intricate.

I am not suggesting that the homilies when held against *Piers Plowman* are in all respects rhetorically lacking. As we have already seen, Aelfric's great contemporary, Bishop Wulfstan, shares Langland's predilection for matched pairs. All of the tenth- and eleventh-century English homilists make some use of this device. In both variety and frequency, however, Langland's usage far surpasses that of his predecessors. Where a substantial portion of Langland's pairs are redundant, relatively few are redundant in the homilies as a whole, although among the pairs which are for-mulaic, as will be shown below, the percentage of redundant pairs is higher, and again it is Wulfstan whose usage conforms most closely to that of Langland, though Langland's far surpasses that of his predecessors. Wulfstan, like Langland, was an excitable preacher. Of the homilists, it is in Wulfstan that the largest num-ber of matched pairs is found, and Wulfstan is never seen making deliberate avoidance of a possible matched pair. He seems to share Langland's unrestrained delight in making pairs at every opportunity. Although Wulfstan's homiliary is of considerably less volume than the Vercelli and Blickling, it contains well over one hundred matched pairs to their totals of something less than fifty. Vercelli and Blickling, moreover, set up series which could lend themselves most easily to the creation of additional pairs, but the homilists withstood the temptation. In Vercelli Homily XXXI, for example, the following series of nouns occurs:

riht geleafa *and* gewiss hiht.   *and* fulfremed soð lufu.   *and* þurhwu-nung on godum dædum *and* godnes.   *and* anrædnes.   *and* geþyld. *and* liðnes.   *and* sybb.   *and* hyrsumnes *and* langsumnes.   *and* halig ymbhidignes.   *and* modes bigeng on haligum smeaungum.   *and* clænnes.   *and* mildheortnes.   *and* rihtwisnes.   *and* dryhtnes ege. *and* lufu godcundra þinga.   *and* forhogung hwilwendys wuldres.   *and* gelustfullung þæs heofonlican eðles.   (113r)

There are many such passages in the Vercelli homilies, with long strings of parallel nouns notably lacking in alliteration. In Blickling there seems to be less conscious control of pairing, but several sentences which are formulaic in structure resemble the nonalliterating series in Vercelli. A typical cluster of nouns often found together would be: ". . . on hungre, *and* on þurste, *and* on cyle . . . on gewinne *and* on swate . . . on wope *and* on un-rotnesse *and* on sare . . ." (59).

The portions of other manuscripts containing homilies under present consideration average six matched pairs each—not an impressive figure or, except in a negative sense, a significant one. All contain a few series of nouns or other parts of speech for most of which it seems that mates could easily be found for the formation of matched pairs.

Since we have no way of knowing what remnants of these old homilies may have made their way, buried in thirteenth- and fourteenth-century sermons, into Langland's time, it is more important to view *Piers Plowman* against a background of homilies in general than to compare it with the work of one homilist. As an index to the common practice of homilists who indulged in word-play nothing can serve better than the formula, that key which has in recent years opened such a variety of locks. For the present, any alliterating matched pair may be considered, by stretching the term, formulaic, if it occurs twice in the homilies or if it has the earmarks and the congruence of meaning which are characteristic of its type. (Examples of the latter are: *Sette* and *sealde* [C.C.C.C. 41, 487]; and *to hæle* and *to helpe* [Bl., 105]. These two pairs have probably escaped my notice in other homiliaries;

their simplicity and rhythmic balance would make popularity among medieval audiences inevitable.)

As should be expected after a time lapse of over three hundred years, the vocabulary of Late Middle English has deposited in *Piers Plowman* a collection of formulaic matched pairs quite different from those accumulated by the homilists. Thus far only five which are found in both depositories have come to notice:

caseras and *cyningas* Verc., 70r, Hatt. 114, 107v*,[18] *Piers Plowman*, B XIX, 134 *to hæle* and *to* helpe B 1., 105, *Piers Plowman* B IX, 202 *leoht* and *lif* Jun. 85, 14r, *Piers Plowman*, B IX, 29, XVIII, 59*[18] *wanað* and *weaxeð* Verc., 104r, *Piers Plowman* B VIII, 39, XV, 3* 261,* 267,* B XII, 224, B XIII, 145,* B XIV, 14.*

See the Appendix for specimens of matched pairs which appear twice or more in (a.) the homilies; and (b.) *Piers Plowman.*

The very nature of a matched pair—two nouns, two verbs, and so forth, with *and* as the coupling in most instances—gives it a metrical pattern, usually that of a Sievers A-type of hemistich. (Anacrusis is enlisted where an initial preposition or a prefix or other particle precedes the first alliterating syllable of the pair.) Pairs which follow this pattern and also combine two very closely related words (*reccean* "tell" and *raedan* "advise" [Bl., 111]) can therefore be viewed with some confidence as formulaic, even though present proof is deficient. A number of such pairs are cited in the Appendix.

Only three *annominationes* have been noted as spanning the centuries in the manner of the matched pairs cited above which appeared both in the homilies and in *Piers Plowman: bidde* and *beode,* Wulf., 183; and *Piers Plowman,* B X, 197; *freond* [and] *feond,* AE, 522; and *Piers Plowman,* B XV, 137; *mede* and *mete,* Bodl. 340, 148; and *Piers Plowman,* C VIII, 85.

Against the dense ground of Langland's five hundred and more specimens of *annominatio,* the three dozen which I have detected in the homilies appear as a mere sprinkling, nothing by way of making a pattern. Repetition may enrich a matched pair, one context lending to the pair something which it had wanted before; but surely in an ambitious piece of literature the repetition of puns is deadly. For proof of this, Langland repeats fewer than ten per cent of his *annominationes*. In the homilies, on the other hand, the thirty-five puns (see the tables below) make over seventy appearances. Most of them, unlike Langland's typical *annominatio* but very much like the matched pairs, have the structure and simple obviousness to ensure their being of a formulaic nature. The homilists, then, who, as a group, are inferior to Langland on a creative basis, are also much less interested or much less resourceful in the invention of puns of the two-word variety. The homilists not only pun with consistent infrequency, but they also apparently draw on old stores to a greater extent than does Langland. However, no such comparison of Langland and the homilists should be made without due attention to the essential difference between verse which is strongly alliterative and prose which is never more than moderately alliterative and sometimes not alliterative at all.

A few of Langland's puns have the inevitable ring that is common to matched pairs (*sonde, sonne,* and *see* [B XIX, 74]); nineteen are actually repeated in *Piers Plowman* (see page 143); and a few have distribution in other works: "Wonede in tho wones," *Piers Plowman,* C I, 18, and *Gawain and the Green Knight,* l. 257; "a freke that fre were," *Piers Plowman,* B XIII, 2, and *Gawain,* l. 803; "neghed tho nere," *Piers Plowman,* B XX, 231, and *Gawain,* ll. 697, 929. When all of Langland's unique and heterogeneous puns are surveyed, it is obvious that he prizes originality in word-play more highly than do the homilists.

Predictably, and as we have already noted, Wulfstan most resembles Langland in the making of puns, although Wulfstan favors the formula, both repeating himself and sharing many puns with other homilists. It is true that several of his *annominationes* are found once each in his writings, but even they bear suspicious resemblances to phrases in other homilies. His "gewurde oðð̄e geweorð̄e" (136) is very close to *wære* and *weorþe* (MS U. Lib. Ii.I.33, 209r); "on grið̄e *and* on frið̄e" (Wulfstan 252) is a commonplace redundancy; "man gemanan wið̄ amansode" (205), a triple pun, is like "ma *and* ma mannum gemaene" (191), which is found in the earlier Blickling (11); metathetical "on myrhð̄e . . . on yrmð̄e" (161) may have been inspired by "þa mærþa *and* þa myrhþe" (164, 249, 260, 266, 275; C.C.C.C. 303, 226). "Saca *and* wraca" (223) stands alone, but then so does "sacu *and* clacu" (140).

IV *Intertextual Puns*

In addition to the agglomeration of over fifteen hundred puns and pairs, there is an extension of the function of word-play—a refinement which opens another door to the writer's mind. It may, as a device in its own right, for the time being be called, if not formally christened, "the intertextual pun." For, with what must be the ultimate rhetorical antic in a writer who is an inveterate reviser and punster, Langland makes puns in the C text by substituting nearly homophonous words for key words in B. This gambit is so private, so unlikely of discovery, that we must conclude his own pleasure was *always* a motivation when he played on words; and it may be added that "play" now applies more accurately to William Langland than to any other medieval rhetorician-poet who wrote in English. It is one more paradox in a complex personality, this toying with small forms throughout every phase of the most serious writing a man could attempt. He found relief, then, from the weighty burden of composition; he amused himself at the same time that he was strengthening his lines and emphasizing his points by the addition of puns and pairs; and, beyond the place where utility ends and whimsy rules, there is no way of gauging his secret pleasure. Without benefit of the pun-between-texts, any mention of amusement or humor would be a hazard, the conception of word-play being what it was among all ancient and medieval writers. But, when a poet goes to the trouble of working into his new text a new word bearing marked resemblance to the replaced word from the old text, it is perfectly clear that the pun was made as a private joke; it serves no other purpose.

I believe this entombed pun to be comparatively rare in *Piers Plowman*, but it is possible that I have overlooked many of the type. As with all patterns in this study, scribal interference is a factor whose importance cannot be estimated at this time, although "hard" readings do not seem to have been the cause of variation.[19] When a variant reading in B contains the same form as Langland's supposed revision in C, I regard the form in C as possibly being a scribe's adoption and therefore as not eligible for inclusion among the "intertextual" puns. An example is C II, 39.

Line 38 augments the relevancy of *sueth* in B, since by its use the idea of "following" is sustained. *Seeth* in C agrees with three of Skeat's variants from four B manuscripts. Also, *sueth* fits better with *schendeth* in A than does *seeth*.

> For the fend and they flesch folwen to-gederes,
> And that seeth [schendeth in A] the saule and
>   seith hit the in herte . . .   (C II, 38–39)

The same passage in B:

> For the fende and thi flesch folweth the to-gidere,
> This and that sueth [pursues] thi soule and seith
>   it in thin herte: (B I, 40–41)

(Skeat's footnote: B 41. sueth R: seest L; seeth WO; sees C.) The only consideration in support of *seeth* as Langland's own choice is the fact that *seeth-seith* is more effective word-play than is *sueth-seith*. In any case, *sueth* of B and *seeth* of C cannot be coupled as a BC pun.

Two types of this extension of *annominatio*, the intertextual pun, are distinguishable. In the first, a handful of puns involve two words which are synonymous in a general way. Each of these puns is found within the first eleven passus of C and therefore in the Visio, the part of the poem which was twice rewritten. I—223 *tyliers* (*tolleres*); IV—169 *alle men* (*mynstralles*); 477 *berne* (*baroun*); VII—329 *penaunce* (*penitencia*); VIII—132 *lyght* (syȝte); IX—129 *lorelles* (*loselles*) [actually the same word]; X—44 *plede* (*pleteden*) [also the same word]; 321 *doth wel* (*Dowel*); XI—25 *nat wel* (*yuel*); 41 *fareth* (*falleth*—"befalls").

The second type is the ordinary two-word pun, or *annominatio*. The two words involved seldom have a perceivable direct relationship and, in short, are from the same cloth as the hundreds of *annominationes* already cited. Some of them effect the kind of semantic accretion which I have described. For example, in C III, 206, where the King is speaking of the evil works of False and Liar, "here werkus alle" replaces "worcheth so ille," with *ille* prompting the poet to bring in his favorite adjective. (He removes *al* in two other puns of this type, however: XXI, 98, 276.)

Of itself the plural noun *werkus* stands for evil works exclusively when the reference is to False and Liar; *werkus alle* therefore means "all ill works." Some of the puns are the tortured kind over which we grimace today to conceal our pleasure; for example, "thei bysouhte" (C VII, 387) in place of "bi the southe." Word-play covers all three words of the phrase in B. In a single text the pun would seem to be play for the sake of play; as Langland's secret joke in two texts, it helps to correct the unfair but often painted portrait of Langland as a man of gloom.

Another pun (C III, 14) is an ordinary one, but there is a rationale behind it. The adjective *red* had been used of Meed, that scarlet woman, four times within five lines in B. Langland retains only one such adjective in C, which redundantly describes Meed's rubies. The color red is on Langland's mind, and though he is determined to reduce it, probably so that more attention will be drawn by crown, rings, and robe, he still retains the form of the word by inserting the verb *rede* where the adjective *red* was found in B. For the remainder of these puns, any attempt at logical explanation would have to be a strained one. *A-lowed* (C XII, 34) for *loued* may be simple accident.

The only thing to be said certainly, and it hardly needs saying again, would be that it gave Langland a little pleasure to hear the echo, and the same is true of the samples that follow (Items in parentheses are from B.):

C II—140 leue (lede); III—14 rede (red); 150 en-ioynen (ioigned); 177 shope . . . sholde (shodde); 474 recorde (rewarde); VII—387 thei bysouthe (bi the southe); VIII—204 wol (wel); IX—35 ouermore (of more); 66 weden (wende); 129 lorelles (loseles); 307 barnes (bran); X—42 preyde (preyseden); [plede (pleteden) in 44 has only a variant spelling phonemically too close for inclusion here.] XI—71 Wille (wel); XII—2 lif (liche); 34 a-lowed (loued); 87 Semynge (In signe); 126 compas (compassed) [denotations are quite different]; 132 sothfast (sotyle); 133 by-leyue (loue); XIII—39 labbe (laude), out (nou3t); XVI—105 talke (take); XVII—328 thouht (3outhe); 342 self (sylke); XXI—98 falle (alle); 276 helle (alle); 379 dedliche (dede); 427 other Iuwise [Jews] (or otherwise); 444 kyn (kynde); XXII—94 Eorthliche (Thre yliche); 117 onliche (holy); 118 fauntekyn (faunt fyn); 182 thouhte (tau3te); 280 kele ["cool"] (kepe); 295 plede (playeth); 316 for-thi (worthy); XXIII—23 by-fore (by fer); 54 Turned tyte (Torned it); 67 gyle (while); 105 Sounede

(Swouned); 117 brode (blody); 127 pressede on the pope (preched to the peple); 377 adreynt (and dremeth).

V Rhythm and Sound Patterns

The music of *Piers Plowman* is created in diverse ways, most of which can be easily assimilated by a reader untrained in medieval English. The technical question of meter, however, is so complex that thorough analysis would require a separate treatment and would borrow from the theorists of Old English as well as Middle English versification.[20] Such a study, when it arrives, will have a hearty welcome. But an introduction can only deal broadly with rhythm and sound patterns and thereby re-create auditory impacts in a general way. I hope with the illustrations below to provide a start for the reader concerned with linear structure as well as with Langland's ideas.

The rhythm of the poem is loose but regular. In each hemistich of a line there are two or more beats or stresses, usually on alliterating syllables. The first, or "a," hemistich tends to be longer and to receive more stresses than does "b." Likelihood of this pattern is increased when the line begins with a stressed syllable, even in a relatively short hemistich such as "Spynnen, and spek of god" (C IV, 466), where God is not to be demoted to an unstressed syllable. An eight-line description of a chance pilgrim is more or less typical. It also exemplifies the effect often gained in a sentence of some length, where the nouns in series bear the whole in a smooth, swinging motion.

> He bar a bordon [staff] ybounde with a brod lyste [strip of
>   cloth],
> In a weythwynde [climbing plant] wyse ywrythe al aboute;
> A bolle [bowl] and a bagge he bar by hus syde
> And an hondred hanypeles [ampullae] on hus hatte seten,
> Signes of Syse [Assisi] and shilles [shells] of Galys [Gallicia],
> And meny crouche [crosses] on hus cloke and keyes of Rome,
> And the fernycle [St. Veronica's handkerchief] by-fore for
>   men sholde knowe,
> And se by hus sygnes wham he souht hadde.
>   (C VIII, 162–69)

In a passage like this one, the rhythm of the long alliterative line is extended through parallelism of nouns. The line as a unit becomes, then, one measure in the long sentence. In the sketch above, there is no failure to fill at least the minimal pattern of alliteration, and *b* and *s* are used twice. The beginning sets the tone, with four *b*'s and four *w*'s (but only two stresses in "In a weythwynde wyse").

There are similar constructions with compound verbs. Activa Vita, for example, lists an accumulation of his own deficiencies:

> "Ich can nat tabre ne trompe [play drum or trumpet] ne telle
>   faire gestes
> Farten, ne fithelen [fiddle] at festes, ne harpen,
> Iapen [jest] ne Iogelen [juggle] ne gentelliche pipe,
> Nother sailen [dance] ne sautrien [play psaltery] ne singe with
>   the giterne [guitar]."   (C XVI, 205–8)

These lines are highly symmetrical and have the integrity of a quatrain.

For contrast, there are prose sentences of a rough texture which gives force to the thought. In the following example the *a* hemistich begins and ends with unstressed syllables; *smythie* and *smyte* (a pun) are the only alliterating words. Conscience is speaking against war: "And yf eny man smythie hit [a blade] be smyte ther-with to dethe" (C IV, 480). Some lines are regular, yet have the effect of abruptness. A speaker bursts out with a few syllables; these are separated from the remainder of his speech by a parenthetical phrase:

> "Ye, baw for bookes!" quath on [one] was broken out of helle—
> "Ich, *Troianus,* a trewe knyght ich take witness of a pope,"
>   (C XIII, 74–75)
> "Alas, eye [alas]!" quath Elde and Holynesse bothe,
> "That wit shal turne to wrecchednesse for welthe hath al hus wil!"
>   (C XIII, 1–2)

There is also the equally common construction in which the one who utters the ejaculation is identified and performs some action before continuing with his speech.

> "Peter!" quath a ploughman and putte forth hus hefd,
> "Ich knowe hym as kyndeliche as clerkus don hure bokes."
>   (C VIII, 182–83)

In all such sentences, the exclamatory word, or words, is stronger for being isolated in the line.

Some lines are unusual both for density of alliteration and increment of stresses. As in the already quoted "Signes of Syse and shilles of Galys," there can be alliteration of *s* and *sh*. In the following hemistich, which is a real tongue twister, there are four stresses, providing *shupte* (made) is stressed, as I think it may be: "Shruft shupte sharpe salue" (C XXIII, 306). Sibilants are also effective in more conventional structures. For example, Guile borrowed horses "And shope [arranged] that a shereyue [sheriff] sholde bere Mede / Softliche in saumbury [litter] fram syse [assize] to syse" (C III, 177–78). The impression of the softness of the luxurious lady's comfort is well conveyed. Elsewhere liquids, nasals, glides, vowels, as well as sibilants, alliterate to suggest a gentle or dreamy quality. Ten of the first eleven lines of the poem, for instance, consist entirely of this type of alliteration.

> In a somer seson whan soft was the sonne,
> I shope me in shroudes as I a shepe were,
> In habite as an heremite vnholy of workes,
> Went wyde in this world wondres to here.
> Ac on a May mornynge on Maluerne hulles
> Me byfel a ferly [wonder] of fairy me thouȝte;
> I was wery forwandred and went me to reste
> Vnder a brode banke bi a bornes side,
> And as I lay and lened and loked in the wateres,
> I slombred in a slepyng it sweyued [rippled] so
>   merye.
> Thanne gan I to meten [dream] a merueilouse
>   sweuene [dream],

One consonant may serve in several consecutive lines. In a dialogue with Hope in which he shows how the human hand is like the deity, the Dreamer has already alliterated with *f* in lines 120 and 124. He continues:

> "A fust with a fynger and a foll paume.
> And as the fust is ful hand yfolde to-gederes,
> So is the fader a ful god the furste of hem alle.
> And as my fust is furst er ich my fyngers shewe,
> So is he fader and former the furste of alle thynges;"
>   (C XX, 129–33)

A very different effect is provided by strings of the voiceless stops *t* and *k*. Meed's easy fickleness is described thus: "For hue [she] ys tykel [wanton] of hure tail talewys [slanderous] of tonge, / As comune as the cart-wey to knaues and to alle," (C IV, 167–68). The effect is one of speed—in this case, rapidity of change.

Driveling and gnawing (initial *g* sound in Middle English) are audible in the following: "Thus thei [the ignorant] dreuelen atte deyes [dais] the deyte [deity] to know, / And gnawen god with gorge when here guttes fullen" (C XII, 40–41). The *k* of cursing is similarly used:

> Wysdom and wit now is nat worth a carse
> Bote [unless] hit [they] be carded with couetyse as clothers kemben wolle.
> Ho that [whoever] can contreeue and caste to deceyue the puple,
> And lette [hinder] with a loueday [arbitration day] treuthe, and by-gyle hym,
> That can coueite and caste thus aren cleped in-to counsail.
> (C XII, 14–18)

Here it will be noted that *carse* in 14 sets up the alliteration of 15, 16, and 18. This method of blending lines is often used by Langland. Other examples:

> Wasshen wel with water and with taseles [teazles] cracched,
> Ytouked [tucked], and ytented [stretched] and vnder tailloures hande. (B XV, 446–47)
> And presentide hym with pite aperynge by mirre [myrrh];
> For mirre is mercy to mene and mylde speche of tonge.
> (C XXII, 92–93)

Here the first alliterating word with *m* is repeated, somewhat in the manner of stanza connections in *The Pearl*.

In the following the *foules* are embellished by the next line, and the flow of *w* and *f* gives special beauty to the creatures represented. Langland himself was so pleased with "wilde wormes in wodes" that he repeated it in C XVI, 293: "Wilde wormes in wodes and wonderful foules / With fleckede fetheres and of fele [many] colours" (C XIV, 137–38). But the most delightful description of a bird is the comparison of peacock and lark to the disadvantage of the former: "The larke, that is a lasse fowel is loueloker of lydene [voice], / And swettur of sauour and swyfter of wynge" (C XV, 186–87). Langland uses the *l* of larke; and the *a b* double alliteration (line 186) calls our attention to the loveliness of this "lesser fowl." *Loueloker* attracts more stress than do any of the other words. The compounded adjectives make for sentiment.

Much more that can barely be touched here needs to be said about linear structure. There are proverbs in new guise more easily remembered. Speakers in every conceivable mood exhaust the types of discourse. A multitude of characters *and* scenes are delineated with almost unfailing distinction. Abstractions are explained through the strumming consonants of concrete nouns. Remarkably, these and all of the machinery of *Piers Plowman* are maintained by the four or five threads of primary and secondary syllabic stress that drop through the length of the poem.

CHAPTER 7

After the Plowing

PIERS PLOWMAN was a book much read until new modes of literature swept in with the Renaissance. Then for three centuries it was almost undisturbed, and when a revival of sorts occurred in the nineteenth century the re-discoverers of the poem were not the common folk who had helped fill William Langland's audience. They were, out of linguistic necessity, philologists for whom, both as teachers and writers, the poem was to become valuable material. They and their successors have approached it as sermon and as allegory, as epitome of literary lore and as theological tome, as rhetorical sampler and specimen of Late Middle English.

The Canterbury Tales have also been studied for a variety of scholarly reasons, but the tales have been read for pleasure as well by very many of the legions to whom Chaucer, at first an assignment or a curiosity, developed into a storytelling personality whom there was no resisting. Chaucer seduces readers who respond to epigrams that stick, to intimate nudges, to once-upon-a-time tales of fast action or naughty wenches or marvels strange to English ears. A virtuoso who glories in exercising and displaying his craft, he assures for himself the attention of *vulgus mobile* by all but exhausting the available genres of Western literature in his restless experiments.

I am not going to suggest that *Piers Plowman* approaches Chaucer's works in these respects. Certainly the critics of *Piers Plowman* have, in their silence on the subject of audience appeal, left no doubt that Langland has limitations. To speak of him is to speak of a poet who is first a missionary, then a contemplative, then a sociologist—and who is also a writer because he will reach the largest possible number of the weak and wandering. The majority of his critics commend him greatly but regret his failures as an artist. They speak of the lack of unity and poetic sensibility, and they wish that in his labors he had brought the C version nearer to structural perfection. When he is commended, it is for his passion of conviction, the strength of which must have given him a compulsion to study the mysteries that trouble us all. And he must have studied in solitude for the greater part of his life, for he attained a level of scholarship rare even among our great poets. He seems to me to be more impressive in this regard than, for example, Chaucer, Shakespeare, Pope, Whitman, and Frost.

As we have already seen, Langland is praised for the uniquely masterful synthesis of classical, patristic, and medieval lore which constitutes *Piers Plowman* and for the breadth of his vision. Excepting the mystics, who have not his stories to tell nor his complaints to shout, he is alone and centuries ahead of his time as one whose writings are directly autobiographical. The power of the man could not be throttled by mere convention; in point after point we see him shrugging or wrenching off the shackles of the Middle Ages and producing a work that, as an anatomy, is Renaissance but, as autobiography, strictly modern.

His editors and the analysts of his allegory and language have, I think, been fair to him as far as they have gone. But he has received few words of thanks from the thousands to whom he has provided *entertainment,* and in their silence on this sole aspect of his poem is to be found the most serious oversight in his critical reception. All the other writers of his rank have from their beginnings been applauded as public performers, *pleasers* of the crowd, good company for the hours of leisure. And undoubtedly in his own beginnings and for a while after, Will Langland was most kindly and warmly thought of—most gratefully remembered for the lives he had enriched, for the bite and balm of his stirring lines. He had sung better to the commoners, in some ways, than their balladmakers had sung: he had voiced their woes and their worries as no one had done before; with a work of great substance and beauty he had done honor to the poorest; and we think today that large numbers of his countrymen read his lines and heard them. If they did, Langland must have held a high place in their minds as a supplier of entertainment.[1]

Not so today. Today, as I have said, *Piers Plowman* is dissected over and over, and its meanings are progressively more fully understood. But Langland himself is often called a gloomy man with unorthodox and seemingly illogical ideas about writing on his chosen subject of salvation, and so, scarcely anyone pretends to be drawn to him as a personality, and his poem is found to be oddly linked in its parts and indefinite in its central messages. It is, therefore, not surprising that modern readers, whom *Piers Plowman* can never seduce as *The Canterbury Tales* has done, tend not to think of Langland's work as a form of entertainment.

I *Modern Appeal*

Yet, at no risk of falling into intentional fallacy, it can be asserted that in its author's mind *Piers Plowman* was a most cunning pastiche of the kind of characters who did the sorts of things (described in pungent phrases) that would delight, nay enchant, the interested Englishman of the fourteenth century. And surely in its gusto and its pricking truths, it still has fascination for modern readers possessing some competence in Middle English. It is, after all, nearer to us in time than are Aristophanes' unfading phantasmagoria and the frequently re-translated and re-issued *The Divine Comedy*. Even in translation (the only way most of us read our Greeks and Italians), many of the qualities discussed in this study are more or less preserved. Most serious of the losses through translation of Middle English are in structure and idiom, but though vestiges of the original do linger in modern English, the truth remains that *Piers Plowman* should be read in Middle English. I argued in an earlier chapter that, while Langland has a slightly higher percentage than Chaucer of foreign words, Langland is seldom more difficult to read than Chaucer.

Chaucer, the darling of advanced students and even of some surprised beginners, insinuates his art in the time-honored manner of great storytellers. Now, stories are one means of getting an audience for oneself, and songs, for that matter, are another; and who is to say that Chaucer and Langland and any other metrical poet are not singers? Singers both, Chaucer and Langland make their appeals by using quite different techniques. Where Chaucer has adhesive couplets with many a truism and proverb tucked in, Langland has outbursts of several lines. Where Chaucer leans forward with a "Now you see, my friend, this is the way it was," Langland keeps his distance, as an orator should; and to think of Langland mounted in a pulpit is not an incongruity. Where Chaucer's characters would be easy choices in a police lineup, Langland's are semi-abstractions (not including the Seven Sins), and their natures shift and metamorphose in dreamlike fashion. The ones I mean are, of course, Do-wel, Do-bet, Do-best and Anima, Activa Vita, Lady Meed, Lady Holychurch, the Dreamer, and Piers himself. Only one of Chaucer's people, the old man of the "Pardoner's Tale," bears resemblance.

In the present age of absurdist, obscurantist, nihilistic antiliterature, we should not be alienated from *Piers Plowman* because of lack of character definition or lack of an orderly plot resolution. Rather, it would seem, we should concede that, in spite of his "unstylish" religious orthodoxy, there is much in Langland's deliberate ambiguity and ellipsis to interest readers today. Even logically he is defensible, dealing as he does with questions that may never be answered by mortals or for them. May it not be said that Langland allowed for a margin of error in setting forth his prescriptions for salvation and in delineating the hero of his saga, if the term may be so loosely used?

II   *A Winding Way*

My own method of showing to my reader elements of interest to us in the twentieth century has taken us on different trails, and it may even be said we have chosen side-paths and spent little time on the rising high road to salvation. To repeat, studies of *Piers Plowman* as pure allegory are already voluminous. However, discussion of the character Langland, as revealed in his own revisions and in studies of his rhetoric, have been sparse and fragmentary. My findings, if they are even conditionally valid, are a small part of a mere beginning in these areas.

In summary, I have first displayed facets of William Langland's personality by reviewing a few apparently reliable known facts, in particular his humble station, his career as "a lone wolf of letters" (a phrase he would approve), his devotion to a single project and his indefatigability in its execution. The relative importance to him of each of the Seven Deadly Sins is clearly implied in the poem.

Cautious comparison of the three texts unearthed a few points of interest. As Langland grew older, he apparently became more loquacious: the lines are longer in C. Judged by his use of adverbs and *-liche*, Langland mellowed in old age but still flamed with intense feeling on occasion. Certainly his attitude toward humanity became more catholic; even the "wicked" fared a little better in his hands. Oddly, the word *heaven* held a stronger attraction for him when he wrote the A and B versions; and, conversely, in C, though he tended to omit oaths where they naturally fit, his vocabulary in general became more, not less, earthy. His passionate feelings against poverty never lessened; official pronouncements on poverty by today's affluent societies are mild indeed when weighed against the protests against poverty that ring through all of his texts.

Word-play analysis brought to view a body of material which is of more use to critics of the poem than to would-be biographers of William Langland. One simple fact was made manifest: the poet regarded by so many for so long as a victim of acute melancholia was actually a man who—irrespective of the season or the year, the rising or falling state of his own spirit or his own fortunes, even the nature of his topic at a given time, regardless therefore of everything that makes one grim—as a matter of habit and nature went right on turning puns and setting words together in pairs because he liked to hear them clink.[2] In so doing, he demonstrated along with the preacher's usual shared interests a trait which runs in thinner vein through the bulk of Old English homilies.

Along with word-play, Langland gives us metaphor (discussed by Skeat, Lawlor, Salter, Kaske, and many others) and a richly imaged world of sounds and colors and contrasting shapes. He gives us what our human nature craves so strongly, change and variety, leaving no space to protracted moralising or overelaborated explanation but always moving on—new faces, new encounters, digressions, broad leaps of imagination. Monotony is no fault of his writing; rather, we might complain that he makes us nervous, this probing, darting, changeable mind. I for one have wished that he might have been just a whit more settled and methodical. But then, changeable as he is, he gives us hope at our worst.

Now, although a spiritual message of hope is not ordinarily thought of as a type of entertainment today, it is a source of cheer if listened to receptively—and a song is the same, and a pun or any other joke that can raise someone's spirits. In time of war (it might be said that to Langland the war never stopped) the very songs a people compose are those of optimism rallying the fighters with assurances that they will succeed. The American Negro song

"We Shall Overcome," which was circulated in 1963, is a good example. It was not, of course, considered entertaining by some; and *Piers Plowman*'s message of hope has fallen on many a deaf ear, but for those who are anxious about eternity its words are sure to have a pleasant effect.

This is not to say that *Piers Plowman* is a devotional for the use of the faithful which contains nothing of stimulation for anyone else. Langland's delineation of himself is alone enough to captivate the reader uninterested in questions of religion. It is exciting just to follow him through the pilgrimage which was his life—to spy, sometimes through chinks between his lines, this comical and impressive man flinging himself along a crowded street, his long, bony frame lost in the shabby cloak that flaps about him, twisting his neck this way and that as his poet's eye records a myriad of details in the scene he is passing through. Now his hands are pressed in prayer; now they clasp the arm of an old friend, another saint or a rogue; now they reach forth eagerly for an offered drink. We see him almost distracted, having visions one moment and invitations to sin the next, even the wasting of an hour being to this restless, driving man a sin of a kind.

To make his acquaintance in this manner, to find a writer who surges up from his pages to meet us and then becomes our friend forever is, if we speak of entertainment, the best experience a lyric poem or a story can afford. The degree of intimacy of the self-revelation is up to the writer. Some writers stay closed up; we never know them. Some tell everything, so that after a little we begin to be bored. Langland is generous with us. I think he gives all we need to know, and even in his relative taciturnity there is something to be respected. It is a masculine quality, which is suggested by the texture of his verse, a man's choice of images, bluntness, raw power. Then we remember the conditions in which he lived and wrote, the sacrifices his writing must have required, a vision that surpassed mortality, and his thirty years of trying to encompass it.

Appendix

Chapter Three
(Notes are provided where other readings are found in George Kane's *Piers Plowman: The A Version* [New York, 1960].)

B Prol.—X

Additions in B of *al* as adjective (over A) (one or more lines): B Prol.—103, 119, 153, 175, 177, 179, 181, 183, 186, 187, 194, 196; I—148; II—29, 55, 85, 86, 87, 93, 173, 205; III—56, 163; IV—39, 115, 157; V—11, 90, 106, 150, 161, 180, 181, 237, 240, 277, 289, 290, 416, 485, 486, 487, 490, 503, 516; VII—77, 146; IX—15, 82, 87, 104; X—76, 231, 243, 245, 267, 269, 279, 280, 326, 358, 430, 436, 447.

Deletions in B of *al* as adjective (from A) (one or more lines): A II—48 (Kane *deest*), 68, 159; III—55, 256; (Kane *deest*) VII—172; VIII—58; X—34, 84, 157, 195; XI—217, 265.

Additions in C of *al* as adjective (over B) (short emendations): C I—100, 104, 121, 144; II—17, 75, 199, 200; III—119, 206; IV—422; V—76, 98, 119, 180; VI—126, 140, 148, 169; VII—138, 287, 437 (2); VIII—190, 206, 250; IX—57, 66, 96, 110, 205; X—20; XI—67, 82, 104, 300; XII—25, 214, 223, 245, 280.

Additions in C of *al* as adjective (over B) (one or more lines): C I—100, 104, 121; II—120; III—32, 47; IV—104, 107, 143, 212, 235, 252, 341, 364, 366, 374 (2), 375, 380, 388, 389, 400, 468; V—121, 181, 182, 186, 195; VI—88, 99, 101, 114, 126, 183, 191, 194, 197; VII—13, 18, 26, 39, 64, 110, 114, 115, 142, 256, 336, 337, 424; VIII—216, 250, 258, 259; IX—197, 200, 216, 251, 261, 283, 285; X—43, 57, 128, 165, 178, 187, 201, 219, 260, 264; XI—179, 190; XII—95, 155, 201, 227; XIII—18.

Deletions in C of *al* as adjective (from B) (short emendations): C III—90, 166; IV—13; V—39, 157, 164; VI—112, 199; VII—32, 136; VIII—126; IX—239; X—172, 300, 323; XII—151, 212, 220.

Deletions in C of *al* as adjective (from B) (one or more lines): B Prol.—143, 194, 196, 222; I—131, 133; II—29, 44, 172; V—106, 111, 119, 237, 289; VII—15; IX—15, 40, 48, 82, 87, 104; X—16, 103,

214, 231, 267, 269, 279, 280, 358, 430, 436, 440, 447; XI—50, 164, 172.

B XI–XX C XIII–XXIII

Additions of *al* as adjective in B: B XI—20, 42, 50, 60, 97, 114, 118, 139, 164, 172, 205, 212, 219, 234, 247, 289, 312, 326, 334, 361; XII—46, 110, 130, 137, 156, 216, 246, 249, 256, 275; XIII—39, 69, 123, 124, 143, 144, 154, 167, 169, 171, 173, 197, 208, 209, 225, 239, 252, 264, 280, 350, 366; XIV—17, 37, 45, 54, 117, 148, 176, 184, 194, 202, 223, 258, 259, 276, 295, 298, 299, 318; XV—30, 33, 39, 45, 48 (2), 52, 67, 92, 156, 164 (2), 169, 184, 208, 244, 254, 255, 266, 291, 298, 337, 374, 430, 432, 438, 474, 476, 523, 532, 553 (2), 555, 591; XVI—11, 21, 41, 57, 130, 133, 163, 184, 190, 252, 267, 271; XVII—3, 14, 27, 35, 37, 97, 116, 119, 120, 127, 129 (2), 151, 156, 159, 161, 168, 175, 194, 210, 246 (2), 249, 252, 301, 305, 312, 343, 347; XVIII—39, 44, 61, 83, 94, 99, 107, 174, 213, 223 (2), 235, 253, 254, 255, 263, 265, 269, 308, 310, 316, 326, 332, 342, 348, 370, 374, 383, 387, 394, 395, 402, 403, 415; XIX—8, 17, 21, 25, 56, 77, 78, 92, 103, 148, 158, 161, 169, 174, 179, 180, 185, 197, 198, 201, 211, 214, 243, 245, 261, 267, 324, 333, 351, 352, 358, 361, 364, 389, 395, 423, 425 (2), 426, 436, 445, 453, 471; XX—34, 39, 48, 52, 59, 60, 63, 77, 88, 111, 123, 129, 134, 150, 207, 242, 243, 253, 260, 262, 274, 297, 339, 363, 370, 379.

Additions in C of *al* as adjective (over B): C XIII—149; XIV—162, 201; XV—43, 91, 109, 163, 189; XVI—8, 13, 60, 79, 90, 91, 136, 155, 169, 195, 197, 222, 237, 249, 279, 280, 305; XVII—18, 22, 23, 32, 33, 152, 216, 293, 317, 324, 346; XVIII—33, 36, 50, 128, 141, 144, 237, 238, 240, 242, 249, 276; XIX—5, 15, 57, 72, 102, 159, 181, 201, 217, 219, 223, 227, 238, 239, 241; XX—37 (2), 39, 103, 104, 108, 131, 238, 242; XXI—45, 109, 188, 189, 215, 275, 283, 290, 305, 329, 339, 343, 356, 367, 409, 436; XXII—59, 253.

Additions of *al* as noun in B: B XI—133, 166, 169, 192, 232, 372, 388; XII—31, 45, 47; XIII—170, 189, 291, 312, 324, 420; XIV—115, 146, 153, 195 (2), 263, 318; XV—53, 168, 365, 372, 420, 435, 546, 591; XVI—70, 130, 183, 189, 213, 224 (2), 236; XVII—123, 130, 150, 181, 183, 250, 295, 311; XVIII—18, 30, 32, 98, 158, 190, 210, 236, 278, 329, 339, 356, 357, 375; XIX—127, 244, 248, 249, 260, 263, 286, 290, 305, 312, 390, 437, 458, 467; XX—91, 280, 363.

Additions of *al* as noun in C (over B): C XIII—163; XIV—222; XV—82, 217; XVI—20, 71; XVII—35, 123; XVIII—134, 166; XIX—141, 197; XX—126, 145, 195; XXI—165, 264, 265, 392.

Chapter Six

I. Annominatio

a. Sample puns of special merit or interest

(Notes are provided where other readings are found in George Kane's *Piers Plowman: The A Version* [New York, 1960].)

A	Pr.	2	I *schop* me in-to a schroud a *scheep* as I were;
C	I	18	*Wonede* in tho *wones* and wyckede spiritus.
B	Pr.	72	*Lewed* men *leued* hym wel and lyked his wordes,
C	I	104	That al the *world* be the *wors;* as holy wryt telleth
B	Pr.	129	*Lowed* to speke in latyn—for *lewed* men ne coude
		148	And *comen* to a conseille for here *comune* profit
		158	A raton of *renon* most *renable* of tonge,
		196	The *mase* amonge vs alle thouȝ we *mysse* a schrewe
C	I	227	*Good goos* and grys *go* we dyne, gowe!
A	I	2	And this *feire* feld, ful of folk *feire* I schal ow schewe. (*Kane first* feire *deest*)
		26	That thou *worthe* the *worse* whon thou *worche* scholdest.
B	I	103	And did hem *swere* on here *swerde* to serue trewthe euere.
		108	And ouer his *mene meyne* made hem archangeles,
A	I	131	For to *loue* thi *louerd leuere* than thi-seluen; (*Kane* lord)
B	I	184	That *faith* with-oute the *faite* is riȝte no thinge worthi,
		207	I may no *lenger lenge* the with now loke the owre lorde!
A	II	3	That *bar* the blisful *barn* that bouȝt vs on the roode, (B IX, 163)
		102	Heo mihte *cusse* the kyng for *cosyn,* ȝif heo schulde.
		185	And bad him faste to fle and his *feeres* eke. (*Kane* fle for fer)
		186	Thenne Fals for *fere* fleih to the *freeres,* (A II, 205)
C	III	28	For shal neuere *brere bere beries* as a vyne,
B	II	234	Saue *Mede* the *mayde* na mo durst abide.
A	III	25	The leste *man* of here *mayne* a mutoun of gold.
		126	Heo is tikel of hire *tayl talewys* of hire tonge,
		138	For heo *copeth* the comissarie and *coteth* the clerkes;

		169	Whon ȝe *witen witerliche* wher the wrong lihth.
		193	Dude hem *hoppe* for *hope* to haue me at wille.
		204	To *aliens,* to *alle men* to honoure hem with ȝiftes.
C	IV	366	Alle *kynne kynde* to knowe and to folwe, (374; B IX, 25, 26; B XII, 130; B XV, 52; C XIX, 21)
B	III	322	And what *smyth* that ony *smytheth* be *smyte* ther-with to deth,
B	IV	175	And seide 'thorw ȝowre lawe, as I *leue* I *lese* many chetes;
C	V	49	Bothe my *gees* and my *grys* and my *gras* he taketh,
C	VI	14	*Mowe* other *mowen* other make bond to sheues,
B	V 32–33		And bad *Bette* kut a bow other tweyne, And *bete Betoun* ther-with but if she wolde worche.
A	V	61	As *pale* as a *pelet* in a *palesye* he seemede,
C	VI	52	With-oute bagge other *botel bote* my wombe one.
C	VII	23	Laughynge al *a-loude* for *lewede* men sholde
B	V	162	Of wykked *wordes* I, Wrath here *wortes* i-made,
		195	With an *hode* on his *hed* a lousi hatte aboue,
		205	To *Wy* and to *Wynchestre* I went to the faire, (Graphemic rather than phonemic, this "eye-pun" is an example of a rare type.)
		240	'*Vsedestow* euere *vsurie,*' quod Repentaunce 'in alle thi lyf-tyme?' (B XVIII, 106)
		243	To wey *pens* with a *peys* and pare the heuyest,
		244	And *lene* it for loue of the crosse to *legge* a wedde and *lese* it; (B V, 250)
		261	'I am holden,' quod he, 'as *hende* as *hounde* is in kychyne,
		280	For alle that haue of thi *good* haue *god* my trouthe! (Play on *good-god* occurs more frequently than any other.)
A	V	254	Ak what *fel* of this *feloun* I con not feire schewe,
C	VII	141	Bothe *byte* and *bete* and brynge forth suche thewes,
		193	Whenne ich was old and *hor* and hadde *lore* that kynde,
		326	What *by-fel* of this *felon* ich can nouht faire shewe;
		432	And *spilde* that ich *spele* myghte ich can nouht *speke* for shame
B	V	386	And thanne gan Glotoun *grete* and *gret* doel to make
		398	And *roxed* and *rored* and rutte atte laste.
C	VIII	115	Ther flaterers and *foles* with here *foule* wordes

B	V	503	And blewe alle thi *blissed* in-to the *blisse* of para-dise.
A	VI	12	*Signes* of *Synay* and schelles of Galys; (*Kane* Synay *deest*)
		34	Bothe *i-sowed* his seed and *suwed* his beestes,
		97	Thenne *loke* that thou *loue* him wel and his lawe holde;
B	V	560	He is as *low* as a *lombe* and *loueliche* of speche,
B	VI	39	Loke ʒe *tene* no *tenaunt* but Treuthe wil assent.
		48	That he *worth worthier* sette and with more blisse,
C	IX	46	Other a knyght fro a knaue other a *queyne* fro a queene.
		127	And thauh ʒe *deye* for *deul* and *deuel* haue that recche!
		184	*Spitten* and spradde donge in *despit* of Hunger.
A	VII	167	And with a benene *bat i-bot* hem by-twene, (*Kane* i-bot *deest*)
		183	*Lome* mennes *limes* weore lythet that tyme,
B	VI	243	And *binam* hym his *mnam* for he ne wolde worche,
		300	With grene poret and *pesen* to *poysoun* Hunger thei thouʒte.
A	VII	252	Let not *sir Surfet* sitten at thi bord;
A	VII	296	*Deyne* not to *dyne* a day niht-olde wortes.
C	X	74	That thei with *spynnynge* may spare *spenen* hit in hous-hyre,
		83	The *wo* of these *women* that *wonyeth* in cotes;
		101	*Reccheth* neuere, ʒe *ryche* thauh suche lorelles steruen.
		110	And arn meuynge after the *mone moneyles* thei walke,
		116	To ʒeuen eche a *wyght wit* welthe, and his hele,
		144	*Reste* hym, and *roste* hym and his ryg turne,
		200	And *bryddes* brouhten to some *bred* wherby thei lyueden.
		208	That *faitours* in frere clothynge hadde *fatte* chekus.
		230	Thus it by-longeth for *lorde* for *lered*, and *lewede*,
		273	And the *woole* worth weye *woo* ys *the thenne!*
		⎧ 295	*Meteles* and moneyles on Maluerne hulles,
		⎨ 296	Musyng on this *meteles* a myle-wey ich ʒeode.
		⎩ 297	And meny tymes this *meteles* made me to studie
B	VIII	32	Maketh the *man many* a tyme to falle and to stonde;
		65	And vnder a *lynde* vppon a *launde lened* I a stounde,

		110	'But *Witte* con *wisse* the,' quod Thou3t. 'where tho thre dwelle;
		111	Ellis *wote* I none that can that now is alyue.' (The *witte-wisse* combination appears often.)
		124	Here is *Wille* wolde *ywyte* yif *Witte* couthe teche hym.
B	IX	1	'Sire *Dowel dwelleth*,' quod Witte 'nou3t a day hennes,
A	X	19	Sire *Seowel* and *Seywel* and Herewel the hende,
		52	He *eggeth* the *ei3e*-siht and herynge to goode,
		72	Is *cheef* souereyn of him-self his soule for to 3eme,
		73	And *cheuesschen* him from charge whon he childhode passeth,
		78	To *route* ne to reste ne to *rooten* in the herte;
		89	Bi *counseil* of *Conscience* a-cordynge with holy churche,
		106	Poul the *apostel* in his *pistel* wrot
		113	Beo payed with thi *porcion porore* or ricchore.
		115	For thorw *soffraunce* seo thou miht hou *souereynes* ariseth; (B XI, 370)
		117	And thus of *drede* and his *dede* Dobest aryseth,
		148	That of *Seth* and his suster *seththen* forth coome;
		154	And *seththen Seth* and his suster *sed* weren spoused to Caymes,
B	IX	131	"Swithe go *shape* a *shippe* of *shides* and of bordes. (B X, 400)
		151	And thus thourw cursed *Caym cam* care uppon erthe;
C	XI	54	Rather haue we no *reste* til we *restitue*
C	XI	254	For *good* sholde wedden *good* thauh thei no *good* hadde, (the *good-good* combination appears often)
A	XI	8	With suche *wyse* wordes to *wisse* eny fooles. (B X, 385)
		11	Thei don bot *drauele* theron *draf* weore hem leuere
		51	Neore merci in *mene men* more then in riche, (54)
		122	That eche *wy3t* beo in *wil* his *wit* the to schewe.
B	X	83	And the more he wynneth and *welt welthes* and ricchesse,
		197	For he *bit* vs be as bretheren and *bidde* for owre enemys,
A	XI	128	And alle *musons* in *musyk* I made hire to knowe.

		187	And *seken* out the *seke* and sende hem that hem nedith;
		189	Thus *bed* the Do-*bet* so berith witnesse the sauter;
		207	That out of *couent* and cloistre *coueiten* to libben. (B XI, 76)
		251	To *wyte* what is Do-wel *witterly* in herte;
B	X	282	*Offyn* and *Fynes* [Hophni and Phineas]; for her coueytise,
		400	Tho he *shope* that *shippe* of shides and bordes;
A	XII	31	Of that he wolde *wite wis* him no betere.
		61	I *stode* stille in a *stodie* and stared a-bowte;
		73	For myssyng of *mete* no *mesour* I coude, (C XIV, 189)
B	XI	76	Why ʒowre *couent coueyteth* to confesse and to burye,
B	XI	103	'He *seith sothe*,' quod Scripture tho and skipte an heigh, and preched;
		157	Pulte oute of *pyne* a *paynym* of Rome.
		162	For that is the boke *blessed* of *blisse* and of ioye:—
		163	God *wrouʒt* it and *wrot* hit with his on fynger,
		189	Ac for the *pore* I shal peye and *pure* wel quyte her trauaille, (241; C XVIII, 69)
		212	That *fides sua* shulde *sauen* hir and *saluen* hir of alle synnes.
		266	And is to *mene* to *men* that on this molde lyuen,
		290	That han noyther *kunnynge* ne *kynne* but a croune one,
C	XII	21	He is reuerenced and *robed* that can *robbe* the peuple
C	XIII	207	Than *angeles*—in her *angre* on this wise hem grette,
		223	And that that *rathest* rypeth *roteth* most saunest.
B	XI	355	Many selcouthes I *seygh* ben nought to *seye* nouthe.
		408	Ac whan he mameled aboute *mete* and *entermeted* to knowe
C	XV	20	As, *loreles* to be *lordes* and lewede men techeres,
B	XII	180	In which flode the *fende fondeth* a man hardest; (B XVI, 40)
		183	And as his *lores*-man *leres* hym bileveth and troweth;
C	XV	97	Clerkes knewen the *comete* and *comen* with here presentes,
B	XII	238	And that the fairest *foule foulest* engendreth,
B	XIII	2	And as a *freke* that *fre* were forth gan I walke.

		26	That *lowe louted* and *loueliche* to Scripture.
		44	In a *morter*, post-*mortem* of many bitter peyne,
		73	Ac I wist neuere *freke* that as a *frere* ʒede bifor men on Englisshe
		79	That he *precheth* he *preueth* nouʒt', to Pacience I tolde,
		108	And if ʒe *fare* so in ʒowre *fermorie ferly* me thinketh,
		112	And *preynte* vpon Pacience to *preie* me to be stille,
		161	Ne noither hete, ne *haille* ne non *helle* pouke. (B XIV, 172)
		173	Al the *witt* of this worlde and *wiʒte* mennes strengthe
		181	'For I wil *go* with this *gome* if god will ʒiue me grace,
		184	After *ʒeres ʒyues* of *ʒiftes* or *ʒernen* to *rede redeles?*
		295	And *louelokest* to *loken* on and lelest of werkes,
		340	To the *souter* of *Southwerke* or of Shordyche dame Emme!
		344	With *lykyng* of Lecherye as by *lokyng* of his eye.
		389	As when I *lened* and *leued* it lost or longe ar it were payed.
		408	The whiche is *Sleuthe* so *slow* that may no *slithes* helpe it,
		425	And ʒiueth hem *mete* and *mede* and pore men refuse
		443	For to *solace* ʒoure *soules* suche ministrales to haue; (453)
B	XIV	66	That no *reyne* ne *rone;* thus rede men in bokes
		149	And as an *hyne* that hadde his *hyre* or he bygonne,
		167	And *yliche* witty and wyse if the wel hadde *lyked*.
		171	For may no *derth* ben hem *dere* drouth, ne weet,
		172	Ne noyther *hete* ne *haille* haue thei *here hele*,
		219	Ne have *powere* in *pouerte* if pacyence it folwe.
		227	For *loulich* he loketh and *loueliche* is his speche,
B	XV	52	It were aʒeynes *kynde*,' quod he 'and *alkynnes* resoun
		53	That any creature shulde *kunne* al excepte Cryste one.
		66	For in the *lykyng* lith a pryde and a *lycames* couetise,
		74	And how that *folke* in *folyes* myspenden her fyue wittes,

		99	Ac there the *rote* is *roten* reson wote the sothe,
		137	To *frende* ne to *fremmed* the *fende* haue his soule!
		139	And that he *spared* and *bispered* spene we in murthe."
		142	Ac for *good men*, *god* wote gret dole *men* maken,
		143	And *bymeneth good* mete-ȝyueres and in mynde haueth,
		147	'Where shulde men fynde such a *frende* with so *fre* an herte?
		151	And wolen *lene* there thei *leue* lelly to ben payed.
		167	Ne no *lykynge* hath to *lye* ne laughe men to scorne.
		172	'Of rentes ne of *ricchesse* ne *reccheth* he neuere.
		181	And whan he is *wery* of that *werke* thanne wil he some tyme
		198	And as a lyoun he *loketh* there men *lakketh* his werkes
		240	For to *wonye* with hem his *wone* was sum tyme,
		270	In *spekes* and in spelonkes selden *speken* togideres.
C	XVIII	24	Bote thre lytel *loues* and *loue* was her souel.
		88	Neither the *see* ne the sande ne the *seed* ȝeldeth
		91	And the *see* and the *seed* the sonne and the mone
B	XV	349	For thorw *werre* and wykked *werkes* and *wederes* vnresonable,
B	XV	425	It is unsauory, for *soth ysothe* or ybake.
C	XVIII	200	And now is reuthe to *rede* hou the *rede* noble
		201	Ys yreuerenced by-fore the *rode* and receyuyd for the worthier
B	XV	527	If *possessioun* be *poysoun* and inparfit hem make,
C	XVIII	235	A-ȝens the *lore* of oure *lorde* as seynt Luk wytnesseth,
		246	And *crye* to *Crist* that he wolde hus coluere sende,
		277	He is a *forbusne* to alle *busshopes* and a bryȝt myrour,
B	XV	573	In *stone*, for it stydfast was and *stonde* sholde euer—
B	XVI	4	'It is a ful *trye tree*,' quod he *trewly* to telle.
		12	Lorde,' quod I, 'if any *wiȝte wyte* whider-out groweth?'
		25	'For wyndes, wiltow *wyte*,' quod he 'to *wi* fram fallynge;
C	XIX	1	'*Leue Liberum Arbitrium*,' quath ich 'ich *l* ich hope,
B	XVI	59	And of o *gretnesse* and *grene* of *greyne* th

60   'That is *soth*,' seide Pieres '*so* it may bifalle; (B XVI, 202)

112   Ofte he *heled* suche he ne *helde* it for no maistrye,

C   XIX   74   As *monkes* and *monyeles* men of holichurche;

92   And *bad* hit be of a *bat* of erthe a man and a mayde;

181   In *inwit* and in alle *wittes* after *Liberum-Arbitrium*

B   XVI   215   That is, *creatour* wex *creature* to knowe what was bothe;

222   And is nouȝt but *gendre* of o *generacioun* bifor Jesu Cryst in heuene,

246   And *defende* hem fro the *fende* folke that on me leueden.

B   XVII   1   'I am *Spes*,' quod he, 'a *spye* and *spire* after a knyȝte,

29   He can nouȝte segge the *somme* and *some* aren in his lappe.

75   And lo here *syluer*,' he seyde 'for *salue* to his woundes.'

C   XX   61   And whanne he hadde *siht* of this *sike asyde* he gan drawe, (63)

68   He *vnbokelede* hus *boteles* and bothe he a-tamede;

B   XVII   96   He shulde stonde and steppe; ac *stalworth worth* he neure,

138   The fader was *fyrst*, as a *fyst* with a fynger foldynge,

C   XX   183   And as glowynge *gledes gladeth* nat these workemen

211   Bote thou haue *tache* to *take* hit with tunder and broches,

300   Hure *fere* fleeth fro huere for *fere* of huere tounge.

B   XVIII   5   And *lened* me to a *lenten* and longe tyme I slepte;

12   Wyth-oute *spores* other *spere* spakliche he loked,

13   As is the *kynde* of a *kynȝte* that cometh to be dubbed, (Note the use of *kynȝte* in order to bring in a pun, and an inferior one at that.)

66   Shal no *wiȝte wite witterly* who shal have the maystrye, (226–27)

86   The blode spronge down by the *spere* and *vnspered* the kniȝtes eyen.

110   What for *fere* of this *ferly* and of the fals Iuwes,

125   'Ich haue *ferly* of this *fare* in feith,' seyde Treuth,

165   'That is *soth*,' seyde Mercy 'and I se here by *southe*,

C   XXI   136   With-oute *wommanes wem* in-to this worlde brouhte hym;

	171	'That is *soth*,' seide Mercy 'and ich seo her by *southe*,
	183	*Moyses* and meny *mo* mercy shullen synge;
	235	To wite what all *wo* is that *wot* of alle ioye;
	239	Ne what is witerliche *wele* til *wele*-a-way hym teche.
B XVIII	247	Lo! helle miȝte nouȝte *holde* but opened tho god *tholed*,
	250	For *Gygas* the geaunt with a *gynne engyned* (See note 11 to Chapter Six.)
	324	And tho that owre lorde loued in-to his *liȝte* he *lauȝte*,
C XXI	284	That *Belial* thy *bel*-syre beot with thy damme,
	287	Cheke we and *cheyne* we and eche *chyne* stoppe,
	288	That no light *leope* yn at louer ne at *loupe*.
	330	'For *god* hath go,' quath Gobelyn 'in a *gome* lyknesse
	414	Til the vendage *valle* in the *vale* of Iosaphat,
B XVIII	396	For I were an *vnkynde kynge* but I my *kynde* holpe,
	404	But *leten* hym *lede* forth what hym lyked and *lete* what hym liste.
C XXI	458	Nother *loue leuere* ne *leuere* freondes,
B XIX	74	Bothe of *sonde, sonne*, and see and sithenes thei went
B XIX	95	As it bicometh a *conquerour* to *konne* many sleightes,
	96	And many *wyles* and witte that *wil* ben a leder;
	104	In his *Iuuente* this Jesus atte *Iuwen* feste
	119	After the kynde that he *come* of there *comsed* he Dowel.
	140	Kepen it fro *niȝt*-comeres with *knyȝtes* y-armed,
	161	And as alle thise *wise wyes* weren togideres,
C XXII	154	The Iuwes *preyede* hem of pees and *preyede* tho knyghtes
	155	Telle the *comune*, that ther *cam* a *companye* of hus aposteles, (And see the following entry.)
	160	In eche *companye* ther heo *cam* '*Christus resurgens*.'
	161	Thus *cam* hit out that Crist ouer-*cam* rekeouered, and lyuede;
	198	And wyckede to *wonye* in *wo* with-outen ende.'
B XIX	197	In *lyknesse* of a *liȝtnynge* he *lyȝte* on hem alle,
	229	And some he *kenned* crafte and *kunnynge* of syȝte,
	234	And some to *dyuyne* and *diuide* noumbres to kenne;
	386	In *helpe* of her *hele* onys in a moneth,

413   For her *pelure* and her palfreyes mete and *piloures*
          that hem folweth.
477   The vyker hadde *fer* home and *faire* toke his leue,
B   XX   46   And suffre *sorwes* ful *sowre* that shal to Ioye tourne."
91   '*Al-arme! alarme!*' quod that lorde 'eche lyf kepe his
          owne!' (Skeat recognizes the pun in *lyf*, ignores
          the pun in the two "alarms.")
133   He Iugged til a *Iustice* and *Iusted* in his ere,
162   This Sleuthe was *war* of *werre* and a slynge made,
231   *Nede neghed* tho *nere* and Conscience he tolde
322   The frere *her-of herde* and hyed faste
384   And sitthe he *gradde* after *grace* til I gan awake.

b. Line numbers of common and largely repetitious puns

A Prol.—6, I—10, 31, II—14, 17, 139 (Kane *deest*), III—47, 229
(Kane 223 *le[n]e*), 256, 262, IV—10 (Kane *man*), 147, 151, V—12,
13, 50, 81, VII—2, 136, VIII—19, 46, IX—59, X—39, 59, 90, 93
(Kane *werchist*), 100, 138, 139, 172, XII—7, 30, 100

B Prol.—49, 197, 207, 210, I—41, 145, II—56, 106, III—104, 234,
243, 244, 276, V—50, 120, 301, 303, 400, 407, 432, 441, 513, VI—
139, 330, VII—17, 135, VIII—533, IX—42, 49, 84, 175, X—2, 7, 24,
61, 80, 109, 189, 252, 263, 265, 345, 346, 356, 385, 438, 446, 455,
XI—35, 62, 76, 162, 163, 171, 370, 375, 416, XII—29, 43, 95, 96, 98,
105, 147, 229, 247, 248, XIII—52, 162, 180, 336, 379, XIV—2, 6, 34,
44, 51, 66, 105, 126, 128, 135, 164, 185, 230, 240, 263, 325, 329,
XV—10, 165, 177, 180, 209, 215, 241, 248, 275, 294, 354, 380, 388,
408, 424, 432, 448, 450, 467, 497, 501, 502, XVI—1, 8, 30, 55, 56,
159, 166, 178, 202, 233, 248, XVII—25, 44, 70, 71, 82, 85, 93, 134,
137, 204, 281, 282, XVIII—56, 89, 98, 106, 177, 195, 207, 215, 223,
246, 265, 344, 411, XIX—91, 150, 193, 236, 237, 303, 323, 397, 398,
407, XX—4, 54, 102, 147, 167, 236, 291, 312, 319, 347

C I—58, 103, II—116, 117, III—75, 78, 101, 122, IV—73, 88, 102,
283, 303, 306, 384, 410, V—31, 163, 190, 191, VI—15, 57, 92, 95,
140, 194, VII—40, 42, 52, 54, 142, 190, 204, 253, 289, 292, 304, 315,
VIII—209, 293, IX—85, 196, XI—39, 51, 79, 200, 208, 211, 220, 238,
258, 267, 310, XII—22, 76, 77, 78, 99, 116, 133, 140, 145, 146, 153,
204, 218, 286, XIII—4, 5, XIV—168, 184, 185, 195, 204, XV—8, 62,
63, 180, 183, XVI—55, 118, 215, XVII—176, 356, XVIII—7, 10, 20,
42, 129, 153, 156, 158, 162, 202, 234, 289, 306, XIX—4, 21, 30, 94,

175, 191, XX—126, 179, 244, 245, 257, XXI—97, 99, 316, 384, 451, XXIII—54, 350

c. *Annominatio* in the Homilies

ætes ne wætes Æ II, 490; Verc. 108r, 112v
bidde *and* beode Wulf., 183
blisse *and* lisse Wulf., 253, 254
mid geferum ferde Æ I, 560
freond *and* feond Æ I, 522
on griðe *and* on friðe Wulf., 252
lara *and* laga Wulf., 176, 200 (2), 201 (2), 225, 237, 253, 256, 269
gelaðað *and* gelædað C.C.C.C. 41, 416
lað *and* lare Wulf., 256; Jun. 85. 14r
forloren *and* forlogen Wulf., 258
forlæran *and* eac forlædan Jun. 85, 14v; Wulf., 190; Verc., 93v
lufian *and* gelyfan Wulf., 164*, 165*, 226; Bl., 17, 25, 111; C.C.C.C.
    162, 439; Faust. A IX, 118r*; Hatt. 114, 110v*; Hatt. 115, 103v*;
    Bodl. 340, 149v*
gelyfað . . . lif Hatt. 115, 103v
ma *and* mannum gemæne Wulf., 191; Bl., 11
man gemanan wið amansode Wulf., 205
þa mærþa *and* þa myrhþe Wulf., 164, 249, 260, 266, 275; C.C.C.C.
    303, 226
on myrhðe *and* yrmðe Wulf., 161
mede *and* mete Bodl. 340, 148
rædan *and* aræran Wulf., 253
rice . . . on his rice Æ I, 460
saca *and* wraca Wulf., 223
sacu *and* clacu Wulf., 140
sincan *and* swincan Verc., 67v
sorgung *and* sargung Wulf., 230
swicole *and* ficole Wulf., 135
he underðeodde ðeoda Æ I, 578
wanað *and* . . . wacað Verc., 104r
wanung *and* granung Wulf., 230
wecst *and* weccest Verc., 134v
weorðian *and* werian Wulf., 202
weorðmynde on munde Verc., 80r
werie *and* nerie Wulf., 208
wide *and* side Wulf., 136, 137, 140, 259, 265; Hatt. 114, 98r
gewurde oððe geweorðe Wulf., 136
wyrdan *and* scyrdan Wulf., 277, 202*

II. *Alliterating Matched Pairs*

a. Matched pairs which appear twice or more in the homilies

to broðrum and to bearnum Bod. 340, 88, 90, 150
caseras *and* cyningas Verc., 70r; Hatt. 114, 107v
clypigende and cweðende Æ. I, 594, 596; Bl. 81; C.C.C.C. 41, 415,
    Jun. 121, 152r (2); Bod. 340, 126v; Jun. 85, 12r
gedreht *and* gedrefed Wulf., 155; Verc., 135v
dumbe and deafe Æ I, 292; II, 436; Wulf., 159*
earmum and eadigum Æ I, 64; Hatt. 114, 55r; Verc., 112v
fixas and fugelas Æ I, 276; II, 206; Hatt. 114, 102v; Verc., 106v*
to fultume and to frofre Æ I, 14, 196; II, 22*; Bl. 201, 203 (2)
gitsunga and gifornesse Wulf., 183, 203, 258, 264, 272; Verc., 11r,
    116r*
his goda and his gyfena C.C.C.C. 162, 385, 440
habban and healdan Bl., 55 (3); Verc., 112v; Wulf., 186, 218, 236
hehst and halgost Bl., 83; Bod. 340, 144r; C.C.C.C. 41, 280
here and hæte Wulf., 264, 271
here and hunger Wulf., 140, 253, 257, 262, 269
hol and hete Wulf., 140, 257
to hycgan and to hihtan Bod. 340, 147v; Verc., 104v
mid lufe ge mid laþe Bl., 45; Verc., 10r, 67r
lufian and læran Wulf., 193, 209 (2)
magan and moton Bl., 95, 110, 125; C.C.C.C. 162, 546; Hatt. 114,
    102v, 106r (2); C.C.C.C. 303, 226; Verc., 88r*, 89r, 93v, 118v;
    Wulf., 126, 163, 232, 320
mæden and moder Æ I, 74, 354; II, 262, 566
mære and micel Æ II, 20; Wulf., 144*, 177; Verc., 108v
mihte and mægenðrymme Æ I, 610; Verc., 106v*; Wulf., 253 (mægen-
    strengðe)
mod and mægene Bl., 97, 209; C.C.C.C. 162, 546 (2); Wulf., 156,
    165, 172, 174, 181, 231, 258, 264, 272, 273; Verc., 11r, 79v, 116r
morðor and man Verc., 11r, 116r (2); Bod. 340, 147v*; Wulf., 163*,
    192*, 226*, 231*
ge mid muðe ge mid mode Æ II, 20; Wulf., 209*
myngige and manige Bl., 109, 161*, 197; Jun. 85, 25r*
repeð and reafað (ryperas and reaferas) C.C.C.C. 303, 225; Wulf.,
    163, 192, 202, 231, 264, 272, 273
rummode and rihtwise Verc., 12r, 116r
sares and sorge Verc., 10r, 115v; Wulf., 121, 236 (2), 253
sungon and sægdon Bl., 105; C.C.C.C. 41, 485; Wulf., 210, 215
swæcc and stenc Æ II, 550, 554, 562
ðeowian and ðenian Wulf., 193; Jun. 86, 49r

waldend and wyrhta Wulf., 158, 224, 225; Verc. (Andreas), l. 649,
l. 1403
His welan and his wista Bl., 111; Wulf., 252
to weorðienne and to wuldrienne Bl., 197; Bod. 340, 144r; Verc., 94v*
wer and wif Æ II, 8, 372, 552; Bl., 107; U. Lib. Ii l. 33, 207r; Jun. 121,
149r; Jun. 85, 4v, Verc., 71r
wlitig and wynsumlic Bl., 107; Verc., 23r
þurh word and þurh weorc Bl., 35; Hatt. 114, 99v; C.C.C.C. 162, 387;
Verc., 11v, 12r, 116r; Wulf., 202, 210, 247, 259, 275
wuldor and wurðmynt Æ I, 75, 538; II, 424, 460, 548; Bl., 65, 169;
Verc., 12r, 56r, 116v

b. Matched pairs which appear twice or more in *Piers Plowman*

a lycence and a leue B Pr., 85, C VII, 121; A Pr., 82*
Dykers, and deluers A Pr., 102, A VII, 100; A XI, 184
ȝoure masse and ȝoure matynes   C I, 125; A V, 2; B V, 418, 460;
C VII, 282; C X, 228; B XI, 275, 301; B XIII, 396; B XX, 364
myȝt and maystrye   A III, 19 (*Kane deest*); B V, 103*
Barouns and burgeis   A III, 150; A X, 134
Wydwes and wyues   B III, 266; C VII, 143*
wilnen and wolde   C IV, 387; C XIV, 94; B XIV, 173; B XV, 24, 546;
C XIX, 261
In-to sikul or to sithe   B III, 306; C VI, 23
Huntynge or haukynge   B III, 311; C IV, 469*
my gees and my grys   B IV, 51; A VII, 268
a sysoure and a sompnoure   B IV, 167; C XXII, 372
monkes and moniales   C VI, 76; C XIX, 74; B XX, 262
Wepyng and wailynge   C VI, 108; A V, 261
couent and cloistre   C VI, 152; B X, 299
formest and ferst   C VII, 15; B XIX, 116*
Knew and couthe   C VII, 58; B XV, 49; B X, 466*; B XIII, 311*
With lered and with lewede   C VII, 116 (too numerous to list)
the residue and the remenaunt   A V, 240; A VII, 93; B XX, 290
flesche and fissche   B V, 443 (*numerous*)
I dyke and I delue   B V, 552; B VI, 143
benes and bren   B VI, 184; A VII, 270
bidders and beggers   A VII, 202 (*Kane* Bolde beggeris *and* bigge);
A VIII, 68; B VI, 206*; C IX, 210; B XV, 199
Loue hem, and lene hem   A VII, 210; C XIII, 107
coket and cler-matin   A VII, 292; C IX, 327*
begge and bidde   B VI, 239; A VIII, 70; B XI, 269; B XV, 251;
A VII, 224*

plente and pees   C XVIII, 93; B XV, 500
werre and wo   B XV, 504; B XVIII, 412
Patriarkes and prophetes   B XII, 117, 138; B XIII, 428; B XVI, 198,
    251, 256; B XVIII, 138, 144, 268, 321; B XIX, 16
steppe ne stonde   B XVII, 54, 96*
Touchede and tastede   C XX, 122; B XVIII, 84
smoke and smolder   B XVII, 321, 323, 341
smoke and smorthre   C XX, 303, 305
a liðte and a leme   B XVIII, 124, 137
in blode and in baptesme   B XVIII, 375; B XIX, 320*
feueres and fluxes   B XIX, 46; B XX, 80

c. Formulaic matched pairs in the homilies

mid blode *and* mid banum Æ II, 270
agifan *and* agildan Bl., 55
godas *and* gydena Æ I, 426
to hæle *and* to helpe Bl., 105
gehealdan *and* geholpen Wulf., 141
hopodon *and* hyhtan Bl., 87
leoht . . . *and* lif Jun. 85, 14r
leornian . . . *and* læran Bl., 113
reccean *and* rædan Bl., 111
ricum *and* reðum Æ I, 298
sette *and* sealde C.C.C.C. 41, 487
þafode *and* ðolode Wulf., 160
þine ðegnas *and* ðine ðeowan Æ II, 584 (*see* ðeowian and ðenian
    above)
wære *and* weorþe U. Lib. Ii l. 33, 209
wanað *and* weaxeð Verc., 104r

Notes and References

Chapter One

1. Langland's use of foreign words, Latin particularly, exceeds Chaucer's but cannot be called heavy. Langland is partial to macaronic constructions.

2. The Anglo-Saxon homilies, which may be considered in five main groups, are only sporadically alliterative. Aelfric's *Lives of Saints* (some items of which, *e.g.* "Ash-Wednesday" and "On Auguries," are not hagiographical) and Wulfstan's homilies are more alliterative than the homilies in the other groups: Aelfric's Catholic Homilies, the Blickling Homilies, the Vercelli Homilies, and a group of miscellaneous, anonymous homilies now being prepared for publication. See Chapter Six for discussion (Section II, "Alliterating Matched Pairs").

3. The poem has been compared with medieval drama and with pulpit literature by Bloomfield, Owst, Salter, Fowler, *et al.* See bibliography.

4. Since Skeat left little for anyone else to say on the subject, his defense of the name "Will Langland" is still the best we have.

5. A IX, 118; XII, 99, 103; B XV, 148; C II, 5; XI, 71.

6. D. W. Robertson, Jr., and Bernard F. Huppé, *Piers Plowman and Scriptural Tradition* (Princeton, 1951), p. 126.

7. Examples: *Peres the Ploughman's Crede,* ca. 1393; *The Crowned King,* 1415; *The Ploughman's Tale,* sixteenth century. See Parry Stroud, *Stephen Vincent Benét* (New York, 1962), p. 85, on Langland's influence on a modern American.

8. See Robertson and Huppé, *op. cit.;* John Lawlor, *Piers Plowman: An Essay in Criticism* (New York, 1962); David C. Fowler, *Piers Plowman: Literary Relations of the A and B Texts* (Seattle, 1961).

9. John Lawlor discusses the disadvantages of extracting fragments of this or any long, extended allegory and offers convincing explanation of the importance of digesting the allegory as a whole (*op. cit.,* pp. 240–65).

10. For an analysis which emphasizes vagueness of thought as Browning's worst fault, see William M. Ryan, "The Classifications of

Browning's 'Difficult' Vocabulary," *Studies in Philology*, LX (1963), 542–48.

11. Fowler, *op. cit.*, pp. 204–5.

12. Robert W. Frank, Jr., *Piers Plowman and the Scheme of Salvation* (New Haven, 1957).

13. Robertson and Huppé make this comment: "Conventional Scriptural exposition gives the plowman a unique symbolic significance. In Luke 9.62, Christ warns that no one who puts his hand to the plow should look back . . ." (pp. 17–18). At the same time, it must be remembered that "plowman" is a general term similar to "worker" in the Middle Ages.

14. In a single deft stroke (C V, 74) Langland anticipates this line, unforgettably describes Peace, and merges the identities Peace and Piers: "Pees putte forth hus hefd and hus panne blody."

15. In *Wynnere and Wastour*, thriftless squires, the reckless military, etc. are wasters. But in *Piers Plowman* wasters are pillagers, vandals of all sorts.

16. Frank, *op. cit.*, pp. 14–15.

17. Multiple interpretation is possible, as it is with Scripture and all poetry. Critics of *Piers Plowman* have varied in their approaches; at one extreme is R. W. Frank, Jr., with "a literal rather than an allegorical" reading (p. 2); at another extreme are Robertson and Huppé, who follow traditional methods of exegesis, adopting *sententia*, the highest level on which a work may be read; then making three-fold interpretation of this *sentence:* tropological, allegorical, and anagogical (defined on p. 65).

18. Miss Hort explains Piers' development as she thinks it would appear to a medieval audience:

> The medieval reader would be on the lookout for an allegorical meaning, and his mind would be tuned to it. He would not be surprised, when he found that the ploughman had become the Good Samaritan, and the Good Samaritan Christ on his way to Jerusalem putting on the body of Piers in order to save man. . . . There is rather a gradual unfolding of the meaning of the figure of Piers the Plowman than any evolution in the idea, let alone a radical change. What was the hidden meaning in the earlier part of the poem becomes explicit in the latter part.

(*Piers Plowman and Contemporary Religious Thought* [New York, n.d.], pp. 24–25.) Nevill Coghill prefers to say that Jesus *lives* Piers rather than that Jesus *is* Piers. Therefore, according to Coghill, Piers is an emblem of Dowel, Dobet, Dobest. ("The Character of Piers

Plowman considered from the B text," *Medium Aevum,* II [1933], 108.)

19. George Kane's A Version, a model for all editors, was published in 1960 (Athlone Press). The B Version is being prepared by Professors Kane and E. Talbot Donaldson; the C Version by Professor A. G. Mitchell and Dr. G. H. Russell.

20. Translations implicitly concede the futility of any attempt to preserve in modern English the line-structure of *Piers Plowman.* J. F. Goodridge provides an accurate prose modernization with good taste. His introduction is excellent (Penguin, 1959). Arthur Burrell in an older translation in verse uses archaic diction, inflections, and word order but lapses from alliteration in long stretches (Everyman, 1912). D. and R. Attwater provide a verse translation in modern idiom (Everyman, 1957).

21. E. Talbot Donaldson, *Piers Plowman: The C-Text and Its Poet* (New Haven, 1949).

Chapter Two

1. John M. Manly, Edith Rickert, Martin M. Crow, Clair C. Olson, and Lilian J. Redstone searched long and diligently in gathering Chaucer's Life Records, which reached the publication stage at the time when my *William Langland* was also on its way to the printer.

2. A C text manuscript in Trinity College, Dublin, names William de Langlond as the son of Stacy de Rokayle.

3. Morton W. Bloomfield, *Piers Plowman as a Fourteenth Century Apocalypse* (New Brunswick, 1961), pp. 162–63. Whatever Langland's ecclesiastical role may have been, the fact of it and his performance as a poet prove how ridiculous was G. L. Kittredge's remark that, if Chaucer had been forced to take holy orders, ". . . a great poet would have been spoiled to make an indifferent parson . . . he would not have comprehended the world . . ." (*Chaucer and His Poetry* [Harvard, 1915], p. 5).

4. For the critic who must depend for the present time on Skeat, there is encouragement in Professor Kane's remarks concerning the need for interpretative criticism and those of A. C. Spearing, who quotes Kane in "Verbal Repetition in *Piers Plowman* B and C," *Journal of English and Germanic Philology,* LXII (1963), 722–37.

5. Donaldson, *op. cit.,* pp. 22, 61.

6. *Ibid.,* p. 76.

7. *Ibid.,* pp. 2–13.

8. See Bernard F. Huppé, *"Petrus, id est Christus:* Word Play in *Piers Plowman,* the B Text," *Journal of English Literary History,* XVII (1950), 163–90; and John Lawlor, *op. cit.,* pp. 265–74.

9. In recent years, only David C. Fowler has persevered in expressing strong doubt that William Langland wrote the poem in all three of its versions. D. W. Robertson, Jr., B. F. Huppé, and R. W. Frank, Jr., imply a degree of doubtfulness by scrupulously referring to "the poet" and "the dreamer," avoiding the name that now appears in most of the indexes of books written about the poem. Frank does state in a footnote that "I myself believe William Langland wrote *Piers Plowman*" (p. 5).

With the publication of George Kane's *Piers Plowman: The Evidence for Authorship* (London, 1965), it seems to me that the long dispute is at an end. It is hardly conceivable that either facts or logic will be brought forth to refute this magnificent defense of the argument for single authorship. Professor Kane gives sympathetic consideration to the claims for multiple authorship, then gently sets them aside. His own case is moved scrupulously step by step, neither gathering up "declarations of faith" which stem from "the unfolding of one man's artistic and spiritual career in the successive forms and content of this poetry" (p. 4), nor overestimating the importance of the meager external evidence that points toward single authorship. At the end of a brilliant presentation, having convinced all reasonable men, he speaks very pointedly of "the direction of the evidence," of which he says that "the three forms of the poem are records of a single writer's successive attempts to realize an imaginative and creative experience."

10. See Chapter 6 below.

Chapter Three

1. A Scottish clergyman, the Rev. Andrew Morton, believes that he has proved, through a count of St. Paul's use of *kai*, that Paul wrote only four of the "Pauline" letters.

2. "Number" is presented as a pattern in a separate section below. Langland's growing inclination to include all people invites comparison with the early liturgical practice (in the fore-Mass and in ancient Masses of the first four centuries) of praying for all people. This is preserved in the Good Friday service of prayer and reading today.

3. In C XX, 182 *lycame* replaces *loue*.

4. When Professor Donaldson says that A is more earthy than the other versions he is, I think, using the term in the completely positive sense of "nature-loving."

5. See Chapter XX of G. G. Coulton's *Chaucer and His England* (London, 1950) for an interesting discussion of the abuses of the poor. Coulton quotes from *Piers Plowman*.

6. Poverty was a theme common to many contemporary poems, such as Chaucer's *Parson's Tale*, Gower's *Vox Clamantis*, pieces by Gower

and others in *Political Poems and Songs Relating to English History* (Rolls Series, 1859–1861) and *Political Songs of England* (Camden Society, 1839). In being less interested in the suffering masses than in the individual poor man, Chaucer and Gower (whose couplets would appeal most strongly to the upper class) showed themselves different from Langland.

7. The modern writer who has made poverty a theme in sentences and lines that survive comparison with Langland's is Edward Dahlberg. His works are also eccentric in this age of mixed conformity and nihilism, and there can be no question that his love for the humble poor is as deep as his hatred for their exploiters. Like Langland, he plays upon the words *poor, impoverish,* and *poverty;* and particularly in his important social novel *Bottom Dogs* (1929), in the essays in *The Sorrows of Priapus* (1957), and in *Because I Was Flesh* (1963), his thoughts are galled by economic injustice.

A more popular but, as time will prove, less durable yet worthy American writer, Edward Wallant, made a beginning of an anatomy of poverty but died at thirty-six. Of his three novels the third, *The Tenants of Moonbloom* (1962), most resembles our medieval treatment of poverty (the slum is its setting) and of the triumph of grace over suffering and squalor.

Chapter Four

1. Frank, *op. cit.*

2. G. R. Owst, *Preaching in Mediaeval England* (New York, 1926); *Literature and Pulpit in Mediaeval England* (New York, 1933).

3. H. W. Wells, "The Philosophy of *Piers Plowman,*" *Publications of the Modern Language Association of America,* LIII (1938), 339.

4. Coghill, *op. cit.*

5. T. P. Dunning, *Piers Plowman: An Interpretation of the A-text* (London, 1937).

6. Bloomfield, *Apocalypse.*

7. Willi Erzgräber, *William Langlands "Piers Plowman": Eine Interpretation des C-Textes* (Heidelberg, 1957).

8. Donaldson, *op. cit.*

9. Elizabeth Salter, *Piers Plowman: An Introduction* (Cambridge, Mass., 1962).

10. Robertson and Huppé, *op. cit.,* p. 3.

11. See Robertson and Huppé, pp. 50–52 *et al.*

12. *Ibid.;* this contrast is illuminated on pp. 50–55.

13. The persuasions of *myry speche* in C (III, 161), replace the force of *maken at my wille* in B (II, 147). This emendation, like the

copious examples in Chapter Three, suggests easing of Langland's intensity as he worked into old age.

14. Secundus pastor: "I have oone to my fere [mate] / As sharp as a thystyll, as rugh as a brere; / She is browyd lyke a brystyll with a sowreloten chere;" (ll. 100–102) Mak: "Yit is she a fowll dowse [wench] if ye com nar: / Ther is none that trowse nor knowys a war [worse] . . ." (ll. 247–48).

15. Skeat's account of the historical basis for this speech (C IV, 219–84) is still the most acceptable, though it has been disputed—particularly on the point of the significance of the "dim cloud" in A and B. See Bernard F. Huppé, *Publications of the Modern Language Association of America*, LIV (1939), 37–64; J. A. W. Bennett, *Publications of the Modern Language Association of America*, LVIII (1943), 566–72.

16. Huppé, *loc. cit.*

17. Skeat calls attention to Ovid, who described Envy in the same manner in *Metamorphoses* ii. 775 (Notes, p. 74).

18. Also in line 139. He is a conscious being only when aroused; that is, he exists only in the state of anger. In this singleness of mood he is like Envy but unlike Pride, who makes her confession meekly.

19. *can* is a misprint in Skeat.

20. For fuller appreciation of humor in this passus see Lawlor, pp. 133–34. He speaks of Langland's "sharp sense of the farcical" and "spirit of irreverent fun."

21. *Ibid.*

22. *Lecherie*, for which "lust" is substituted today as the name of the Deadly Sin, is like "gluttony" in dropping its suffix, yet Langland preserves the form *lecherie*. If, on the conversational level, today's usage may be taken as an indicator of historical usage and "lecher" has never had the popularity of "lechery," Langland was merely following the taste of the public in adopting the ever-popular "glutton" and eschewing "lecher," which I believe, though I am only guessing, to have been more rare.

23. Sloth marries Wanhope in the finale.

24. Donaldson, *op. cit.*, p. 147.

Chapter Five

1. See Skeat's Index for complete citations.

2. Skeat's punctuation of this passage in B is to be noted. Whereas A is punctuated in the same manner as C, the construction beginning with *Bakers, bochers* . . . and ending with *dam Emme*, the B version has a period after *craftes*, separating *dykers* and *delueres* from the others.

Baxsteres and brewesteres and bocheres manye,
Wollewebsteres and weueres of lynnen,
Taillours and tynkeres and tolleres [toll-takers] in
    marketes,
Masons and mynours and many other craftes.
Of alkin libbyng laboreres lopen forth somme,
As dykers and delueres that doth here dedes ille . . .
                                        (B Prol., 218–23)

3. The best explanation of alewives' notoriety is to be found in John Skelton's "The Tunnyng of Elynour Rummyng."
4. To Langland, a judge is "rightful" (C XVI, 291). *Iuges,* he says, *wise men ben holde* (C X, 336).
5. In an earlier passage (C VIII, 97–100), *godes mynstrales* are *beggers* and are distinct from *kynges mynstrales.* See the following paragraph in my text.

Chapter Six

1. John M. Manly, *Piers the Plowman and Its Sequences* (E.E.T.S. Orig. Ser., Extra Vol. 135B, 1908), p. 30.
2. Donaldson, *op. cit.,* p. 74. He quotes Theophilus D. Hall, who called the same line "futile and pithless" (*Modern Language Review,* IV [1908], 7).
3. *The Homilies of Wulfstan* (Oxford, 1957), p. 28.
4. Huppé, "Word Play," 163–90. John Lawlor's section on word-play (*Essay*) is largely based on Huppé's article and argues commendably for caution in the interpretation of Langland's puns. Elizabeth Salter's *Piers Plowman: An Introduction* (Cambridge, Mass., 1962), like Lawlor's a book of the general, introductory type, touches briefly on word-play but does not single out the pun as a device. Editors of the poem have noted an occasional pun in passing (*e.g.,* pages 450 and 454 of George Kane's edition of the A version; and pages 86, 144, 182, and 278 of Skeat's notes). Most of the puns to which Skeat draws attention (four in the notes and eleven in the glossary) are not of the type analyzed in the present study.
5. See Ernst R. Curtius, *European Literature and the Latin Middle Ages* (New York, 1953), pp. 278–80, for a classical definition of *annominatio.*
6. Bethurum, *op. cit.,* p. 28.
7. *Ibid.*
8. *Ibid.*
9. *Ibid.,* p. 92.
10. Discussed below in this chapter. The matched pair is briefly

treated by Fr. Klaeber, who calls it a "copulative alliterative phrase" (*Beowulf and The Fight at Finnsburg* [New York, 1950], p. lxvi). Otto Funke's study of alliteration and stress patterns in certain Old English homilies and hagiographical sermons brings into its purview, along with unpaired phrases which far outnumber them, a few matched pairs; but, except for one example of *Reimspiel* and one of *Reimpaar*, Funke disregards the element of word-play ("Alliterierende und Rhythmisierende Prosa in der Älteren Altenglischen Homiletik," *Anglia*, LXXX [1962], 9–36). The term *Paare* is used by him to represent all combinations of alliterating words, just as *pair* may be used in English. Since my present interest is in pairs made up of words of the same part of speech and of the same syntactic function, what Funke in a second article ("Some Remarks on Wulfstan's Prose Rhythm," *English Studies*, XLIII [1962], 311–18) calls "two grammatically equal members," there is need for the more precise if unhandy term "alliterating matched pair."

11. R. E. Kaske describes *Gygas the geaunt* as having ". . . apparent awkwardness and redundancy . . ." ("Gigas the Giant in *Piers Plowman*," *Journal of English and Germanic Philology*, LVI [1957], 177. In its present company the phrase must be construed as intentionally redundant and viewed in the same light as other matched pairs, if it alliterates. Probability is good. (B XVIII, 250.)

12. *Formest and ferst* is an inversion of today's "first and foremost." See William M. Ryan, "Modern Idioms in *Piers Plowman*," *American Speech*, XXXIV (1959), 67.

13. A large portion of this many-paired passus is taken up with Anima's impassioned teaching, to which the pairs lend force and variety of idiom.

14. Homilies herein cited are found (a) in manuscript (Bodley 340, Bodleian, Hatton 114, Bodleian, Junius 85, 86, Bodleian, Junius 121, Bodleian, Corpus Christi College Cambridge 41, 162, 303, Cambridge University Library Ii. l. 33); (b) in fascimile editions (*Il Codice Vercellese*, ed. M. Förster [Roma, 1913]; *The Blickling Homilies*, ed. Rudolph Willard [Early English Manuscripts in Facsimile X, Copenhagen, 1960]; and (c) in printed editions (*The Blickling Homilies*, ed. R. Morris, E.E.T.S. 58, 63, 73 [1874–80]; *The Homilies of the Anglo-Saxon Church* [Aelfric], ed. B. Thorpe [London, 1844–46]; *The Homilies of Wulfstan*, ed. Dorothy Bethurum [Oxford, 1957]). These homiliaries are representative of the corpus of Old English homilies. See N. R. Ker, *Catalogue of Manuscripts Containing Anglo-Saxon* (Oxford, 1957). To save space I have given page and folio numbers without line numbers.

15. G. R. Owst, *Preaching in Mediaeval England* (New York, 1926); *Literature and Pulpit in Mediaeval England* (New York, 1933).

16. Stanley B. Greenfield, *A Critical History of Old English Literature* (New York, 1965), p. 45.

17. G. N. Garmonsway, ed., *Aelfric's Colloquy* (London, 1947), p. 15.

18. Asterisks mark inversions throughout.

19. See G. Kane's Introduction, p. 132 ff., for discussion and examples of "homoeographic substitutions." Professor Kane believes difficulty often motivated scribes to make alterations.

20. Studies of Old English verse are especially to be recommended to the present reader: Eduard Sievers, *Altgermanische Metrik* (Halle, 1893); John Collins Pope, *The Rhythm of Beowulf* (New Haven, 1942); Alan J. Bliss, *An Introduction to Old English Metre* (Oxford, 1962), *The Metre of Beowulf* (Oxford, 1958).

Chapter Seven

1. Owst refers frequently in *Literature and Pulpit in Medieval England* to preachers' forced competition with minstrels and "other entertainers."

2. Willi Erzgräber, in a very sympathetic study, ranks humor first of the qualities of Langland's *Dichterpersönlichkeit, op. cit.* (p. 11). He comments also on Langland's capacity for pity: *Langland ist . . . klandenkend und hellsichtig genug, um zu erkennen, dass diese Sorge einem natürlichen Grundtreib des Menschen entspringt* (p. 55). As I have indicated in earlier chapters, however, Will Langland has not always been so well understood. Within two hundred years of his death he was taken to task by George Puttenham (*ca.* 1589) in these and other words: "He that wrote the Satyr of Piers Ploughman seemed to have bene a malcontent of that time and therefore bent himselfe wholy to taxe the disorders of that age, and specially the pride of the Romane Clergy, of whose fall he seemeth to be a very true Prophet; his verse is but loose meetre, and his termes hard and obscure, so as in them is litle pleasure to be taken." (Quoted from *Elizabethan Critical Essays*, ed. G. Gregory Smith [Oxford, 1904], p. 64.)

Dorothy Chadwick, elsewhere a sound authority on the Middle Ages, could say this in 1922: "The account of society given in *Piers Plowman* is gloomy. The writer obviously wished to expose corruptions rather than to entertain his readers." *Social Life in the Days of Piers Plowman* (Cambridge, 1922), p. 1.

Selected Bibliography

I. PRIMARY SOURCES

1. Editions in Print

The Vision of William Concerning Piers the Plowman, in Three Parallel Texts, ed. W. W. Skeat. 2 vols. Oxford: The Clarendon Press, 1886.

Piers the Plowman: A Critical Edition of the A Version, ed. T. A. Knott and D. C. Fowler. Baltimore: The Johns Hopkins Press, 1952.

Piers Plowman: The A Version, ed. George Kane. New York: Oxford University Press, 1960.

2. Translations

Burrell, Arthur. The Vision of Piers Plowman. New York: E. P. Dutton and Co., 1912. Verse.

Wells, H. W. The Vision of Piers Plowman Newly Rendered into Modern English. London: Sheed and Co., 1935. Verse.

Attwater, D. and R. The Book Concerning Piers the Plowman. New York: E. P. Dutton and Co., 1957. Verse.

Goodridge, J. F. Piers the Plowman. Baltimore: Penguin Books Inc., 1959. Prose.

II. SECONDARY SOURCES

1. Critical studies of Piers Plowman and related works

BETHURUM, DOROTHY, ed. The Homilies of Wulfstan. New York: Oxford University Press, 1957. The book-length introduction contains critical notes which relate neatly to my examination of wordplay in Piers Plowman.

BLOOMFIELD, MORTON W. Piers Plowman as a Fourteenth Century Apocalypse. New Brunswick, N.J.: Rutgers University Press, 1961. An analysis of the structure of Piers Plowman, its roots which grew from monasticism, and Langland's own scholarly make-up. Classifies the poem as apocalypse, but explains that it both departs from the genre and in so doing takes on characteristics of dream narrative, debate, Menippean satire, as well as complaint, commentary, and sermon, each of which overlaps at least one of the other forms. Monastic ideals are shown as a prime influence. Invaluable.

————. "Present State of *Piers Plowman* Studies," *Speculum*, XIV (1939), 215. A masterful summary which undoubtedly spurred *Piers Plowman* scholars by making clear for the first time the directions and cleavages up to the late 1930's; also by hinting at problems most in need of further treatment.

————. "Was William Langland a Benedictine Monk?," *Modern Language Quarterly*, IV (1943), 57. Provocative and unavoidably inconclusive.

BRIGHT, A. H. *New Light on Piers Plowman*. New York: Oxford University Press, 1928. A brief, early defense of single authorship. Interesting topographical data and illustrative plates.

CARNEGY, F. A. R. *An Attempt to Approach the C-text of Piers Plowman*. London: University of London Press, 1934. This book, like Donaldson's and Erzgräber's, is valuable in the search for the older poet both at the height of his powers and in the calmness of eventide.

CHADWICK, DOROTHY. *Social Life in the Days of Piers Plowman*. London: Cambridge University Press, 1922. A shorter study similar to Coulton's, Reinhardt's *et al.*, with the difference that Miss Chadwick's details are selected as background to a specific work of literature.

CHAMBERS, R. W. *Long Will, Dante, and the Righteous Heathen*. London: Oxford University Press, 1924. A comparative study recognizing associations of *Piers Plowman* and *The Divine Comedy* and presenting Langland as a typical medieval writer concerned with the question of salvation outside the Church.

————. *Man's Unconquerable Mind*. London: Jonathan Cape, [1955] 1939. In Chapter 4 Chambers compares *Piers Plowman* and *The Divine Comedy*, discusses alliterative structure and current scholarship, and begins an analysis of Dowel, Dobet, and Dobest. The analysis is continued in Chapter 5. In a discussion of poems which are similar in spirit Chambers writes movingly of the aged Langland.

COGHILL, NEVILL K. "The Character of Piers Plowman Considered from the B-Text," *Medium Aevum*, II (1933), 108. Argues impressively that Piers symbolizes the three ways of life and that his development is to be equated with the divisions into which the poem falls.

DONALDSON, E. TALBOT. *Piers Plowman: The C-Text and Its Poet.*

New Haven, Conn.: Yale University Press, 1949. To the present date the most intensive effort to limn the man Will Langland. Extreme conjectures are avoided, and suggestions of possible new interpretations are the product of close reading and open and reasonable attitudes.

DUNNING, T. P. *Piers Plowman: An Interpretation of the A-text.* London: Longmans, 1937. Using a socioreligious approach, Father Dunning makes orderly presentation of arguments both old and new in explaining the structure of the poem. His attention is fixed primarily on the fair field of folk rather than on the Dreamer.

ERZGRÄBER, WILLI. *William Langlands "Piers Plowman": Eine Interpretation des C-Textes.* Heidelberg: C. Winter, 1957. Rightly considers the C text as an improvement in certain regards. Enforces the theory of Langland's growth as man and as artist. A supplement to E. T. Donaldson (see above).

FOWLER, DAVID C. *Piers Plowman: Literary Relations of the A and B Texts.* Seattle, Wash.: University of Washington Press, 1961. Apart from his stand on authorship (discussed above), Professor Fowler presents a very useful comparison of the A and B texts on grounds other than those which I cover in the present book. His definitions of Dowel, Dobet, and Dobest clarify bothersome obscurities, and he sees the reader safely through Passus B X.

FRANK, ROBERT W., JR. *Piers Plowman and the Scheme of Salvation.* New Haven, Conn.: Yale University Press, 1957. This interesting book leaves the mainstream of *Piers Plowman* criticism to follow the older lead of Otto Mensendieck and to further advance the theory of One Way of Life (instead of the usual three) which, says Frank, is ramified in various ways through the length of the poem.

FUNKE, OTTO. "Alliterierende und Rhythmisierende Prosa in der Älteren Altenglischen Homiletik." *Anglia,* LXXX (1962), 9. Carefully explores musical qualities of Old English prose which have been generally disregarded.

GEROULD, GORDON H. "The Structural Integrity of *Piers Plowman* B," *Studies in Philology,* XLV (1948), 60. This defense of the poem is important for its positive approach, taken at a time when structural unity was being widely held in question.

HORT, GRETA. *Piers Plowman and Contemporary Religious Thought.* New York: Macmillan Co. (n.d.). Speculates cautiously concerning the central meaning. Surveys Langland's "authorities," particularly in theology.

HUPPÉ, BERNARD F. " 'Petrus Id Est Christus': Word Play in *Piers Plowman,* the B-text," *Journal of English Literary History,* XVII

(1950), 163. The pioneer work in the hitherto almost untouched area of Langland's word-play, this article should be basic to similar studies for years to come.

KANE, GEORGE. *Middle English Literature: A Critical Study of the Romances, the Religious Lyrics, Piers Plowman.* London: Methuen and Co. Ltd., 1951. The chapter on *Piers Plowman* is a well-balanced, realistic appraisal addressed to beginning students of the poem. In brief space it ranges from broad perspective to portraits of the man Langland to consideration of difficulties inherent in manifold scribal emendations.

————. *Piers Plowman: The Evidence for Authorship.* London: University of London, Athlone Press, 1965. Incisive, balanced treatment of the authorship question which weighs the best points which have been made on both sides and irrefutably concludes in favor of William Langland.

KASKE, ROBERT E. "The Use of Simple Figures of Speech in *Piers Plowman B;* Study in the Figurative Expression of Ideas and Opinions," *Studies in Philology,* XLVIII (1951), 571. An orderly examination of the types, functions, and distribution of the simple figures of speech used in *Piers Plowman,* this article exalts the poet and serves as a reminder that late Middle English authors had considerable knowledge of rhetoric.

LAWLOR, JOHN. *Piers Plowman: An Essay in Criticism.* New York: Barnes and Noble, 1962. An introduction for uninitiated readers which in its thoughtful and reverent handling offers much enrichment of understanding and appreciation to Middle English scholars as well.

OAKDEN, J. P. *Alliterative Poetry in Middle English.* 2 vols. Manchester: Manchester University Press, 1930–35. The standard work on the Alliterative Revival, with an excellent section on *Piers Plowman.*

OWST, G. R. *Preaching in Mediaeval England.* New York: The Macmillan Co., 1926.

————. *Literature and Pulpit in Mediaeval England.* New York: The Macmillan Co., 1933. Combined, these two books are a unique monument of scholarship in the literature of satire and complaint and in the homily. The reader is warned, however, that Professor Owst's zeal for his lifetime subject sometimes carries beyond the near point of caution his estimation of the importance of the pulpit.

ROBERTSON, D. W., JR. and BERNARD F. HUPPÉ. *Piers Plowman and Scriptural Tradition.* Princeton, N.J.: Princeton University Press, 1951. The authors weave Scriptural parallels into this needed and readable analysis of the B text. Their general approach has been challenged by Bloomfield, then by Fowler.

SALTER, ELIZABETH. *Piers Plowman: An Introduction*. Cambridge, Mass.: Harvard University Press, 1962. Commendable for its dedication to *Piers Plowman* as a work of art.

SWIECZKOWSKI, WALERIAN. *Word Order Patterning in Middle English: A Quantitative Study Based on Piers Plowman and Middle English Sermons*. The Hague: Mouton, 1962. This study will possibly be of interest to future critics utilizing devices and criteria taken from linguistics. It also complements the findings of Owst and my own chapter on the homilies.

WELLS, H. W. "The Construction of *Piers Plowman*," *Publications of the Modern Language Association*, XLIV (1929), 123. A cogent argument for structural unity as a solid underlay in a poem whose superstructure is untidy in many places.

————. "The Philosophy of *Piers Plowman*," *Publications of the Modern Language Association*, LIII (1938), 339. An interpretation of Dowel, Dobet, and Dobest as mental states not experienced by all men in the same degree. The thesis is supported by later commentators.

YUNCK, JOHN A. *The Lineage of Lady Meed*. Notre Dame: University of Notre Dame Press, 1963. A rigidly faithful study of one phenomenon, venality satire conveyed through allegorical figures such as Lady Meed. One of those narrow books which greatly expand their subject.

2. Background materials

BLOOMFIELD, MORTON W. *The Seven Deadly Sins*. East Lansing, Mich.: Michigan State College Press, 1952. Most of the materials contained in this broad study were unknown to Langland, including those which were pre-fourteenth century. The book is, however, of great value to the twentieth-century reader of *Piers Plowman*, who lives in an age when the concept of sin is all but lost. In addition to definitions of evil and of sin, the Seven Deadly Sins are presented as a theme to be found in writings the world over, beginning in the second century B.C. and extending through the fourteenth and fifteenth centuries in English literature.

COULTON, G. G. *Chaucer and His England*. New York: Barnes and Noble, 1963. Chapters 18–23 offer glimpses of the society to which Chaucer and Langland belonged. Similarly helpful are Coulton's *Medieval Village*, and *Chaucer's World*, ed. by Rickert, Crow, and Olson.

————. *Medieval Panorama*. New York: World Publishing Co. (Meridian), 1955. Scrutinizes the lives of people such as Langland knew, with most attention paid to social customs and economic conditions. Coulton also raises occasional points of religious significance and mentions historical events which particularly affected the common folk. Intellectual life and the arts are not given extensive treatment.

CROW, MARTIN M. and CLAIR C. OLSON. *Chaucer Life Records*. Austin, Texas: University of Texas Press, 1966. Not released at the time of the writing of the present book.

PANTIN, W. A. *The English Church in the Fourteenth Century*. Cambridge: Cambridge University Press, 1955. A survey of the clergy in all ranks, with particular attention to the friars, who also are Langland's concern, and to learning. Of special interest to present readers are chapters on religious literature and on fourteenth century mystics who wrote some of it.

SMALLEY, BERYL. *The Study of the Bible in the Middle Ages*. Oxford: Basil Blackwell, 1952. An encyclopedic study of hundreds of exegetes, preachers, teachers, and liturgists whose lives and works do not touch Langland directly but provide his modern reader with an important piece of the background against which he wrote.

Index

Activa Vita. *See* Haukyn
adverbs, 35–46, 108, 126
Aelfric: mentioned by Owst, 109;
    Lives of the Saints, 110, 146 n.
    2; *Catholic Homilies*, 110, 146 n.
    2; contemporary of Wulfstan, 111;
    Aelfric's Colloquy, 154 n. 17
Aelfric's Colloquy. See Aelfric
al, 35, 37–45, 52, 61, 108, 116–17,
    129–30
Alliterative Morte Arthur, The, 13
alliterative revival, 27
Anatomy of Melancholy, The. See
    Burton, Robert
Anglo-Saxon prosody, 13, 23, 118,
    154 n. 20
Anima, 61, 126, 154 n. 11
Antichrist, 44
antithesis, 107
Aristophanes, 125
Attwater, B., 148 n. 20
Attwater, D., 148 n. 20
Augustan period, 110
authorship, 17–18, 32–33, 149 n. 9
avarice, 20–21, 80, 98; Avarice: con-
    fesses, 77; physical description, 77,
    81; compared with Glutton and
    Envy, 77–78, 81; opposes Poverty,
    78; exclusive nature, 80; recalci-
    trance, 82

beggars, 88–89, 92
Bethurum, Dorothy, 101–3, 109,
    152 nn. 6, 7, 8, 9, 153 n. 14
bishops, 91–92, 96
Blickling homilies, 109, 111, 112,
    114, 146 n. 2

Bloomfield, Morton W., 28, 65, 83,
    146 n. 3, 148 n. 3, 150 n. 6
Brinton, Thomas, 109
Bromyard, John, 109
Browning, Robert, 17
Bunyan, John, 14, 17, 19
Burdach, Konrad, 21
Burrell, Arthur, 148 n. 20
Burton, Robert, 23
Butler, Samuel, 14

Candide. See Voltaire
Canterbury Tales, The. See Chaucer,
    Geoffrey
Carlyle, Thomas, 17
Carnegy, F. A. R., 31
Catholic Homilies. See Aelfric
Caxton, William, 56
Chadwick, Dorothy, 154 n. 2
Chambers, R. W., 31
Chaucer, Geoffrey: writer's personal-
    ity, 18; as *persona*, 19; status of
    pentameter couplets today, 24;
    love of life, 47; "Canon's Yeoman's
    Tale," 78; Life Records, 148 n. 1;
    "Parson's Tale," 149 n. 6; com-
    pared with Langland: difficulty
    for modern reader, 13, 125; as
    satirist, 15; volume of criticism
    and extent of influence, 16; as
    artist, 23; tolerance, 49; financial
    returns, 56; treatment of poverty,
    59, 149 n. 6; praised by Dryden,
    65; character delineation, 66, 81,
    126; Lady Meed and the Wife of
    Bath, 68; word-play, 103, 106;
    popularity today, 104, 123, 125;
    scholarship, 124; use of foreign

ful, 35, 37, 38, 39, 40
Funke, Otto, 153 n. 10

Garmonsway, G. N., 154 n. 17
Giant, 16
gluttony, 79, 80, 151 n. 22; Glutton:
    physical description, 50, 81; humor
    of portrait, 77; compared with
    Avarice, 77; confesses, 79, 80, 82–
    83; uniqueness of his name, 79;
    wavering character, 80; sociabil-
    ity compared with Lechery's, 80;
    compared with Chaucer's Miller
    and Merchant, 81; tempted by
    spices, 94
Goodridge, J. F., 148 n. 20
Gower, John, 13, 56; *Vox Clamantis,*
    149 n. 6
great chain of being, 22
Greenfield, Stanley B., 154 n. 16
Guile, 25, 120

Hall, Theophilus D., 152 n. 2
Haukyn (Activa Vita): one element
    in the Vita, 24; ambiguity of the
    personification, 24; distinct from
    Dowel, Dobet, Dobest, 25; physi-
    cal description, 47; lists his own
    deficiencies, 119; abstractness of
    portrait, 126
Henryson, Robert, 56
hermits, 14, 20, 25, 71, 87, 88
heuene, 41, 47, 49, 52, 127
Hoccleve, Thomas, 56
Holy Scripture, 50
Holychurch, Lady: directs the
    Dreamer, 25; allegorical figure,
    64; physical description, 66; con-
    trasted with Lady Meed, 69–70;
    womanly qualities, 70; abstract-
    ness of portrait, 126
Homer, 22
homilies, 13, 109–15, 127, 142, 143,
    145, 146 n. 2, 153 nn. 10, 14
Homilies of Wulfstan, The. See
    Wulfstan
Hope, 120
Hort, Greta, 29, 147 n. 18
Hunger, 95

Huppé, Bernard F., 65, 70, 101,
    102, 146 nn. 6, 8, 147 nn. 13, 17,
    148 n. 8, 149 n. 9, 150 nn. 10, 11,
    12, 151 n. 16, 152 n. 4

Incarnation, The, 21, 22

John of Trevisa, 18
John XXIII, Pope, 20
Jonson, Ben, 78
Joyce, James, 17, 106
jugglers, 94, 95
justices, 69, 71, 152 n. 4

Kane, George, 28, 31, 129, 131, 133,
    140, 143, 144, 148 nn. 19, 4,
    149 n. 9, 152 n. 4, 154 n. 19
Kaske, R. E., 127, 153 n. 11
Kazantzakis, Nikos, 22
Ker, Neil R., 153 n. 14
King: observed by the Dreamer,
    20; summons Lady Meed, 68;
    weakness 70, 71; and Edward III,
    72; speaks against evil, 116
Kittredge, G. L., 148 n. 3
Klaeber, Fr., 153 n. 10

law: divine, 22, 24, 96; ecclesiastical,
    95; civil, 17, 69, 71, 91, 95, 96;
    human, 96
Lawlor, John, 22, 26, 77, 78, 127,
    146 nn. 8, 9, 148 n. 8, 151 nn. 20,
    21, 152 n. 4
lawyers, 91, 96
Lazarillo de Tormes, 78
lechery, 50, 51, 68, 80; Lechery:
    confesses, 76; sociability compared
    with Glutton's, 80; form of word
    contrasted with *Glutton,* 151 n.
    22
levels of meaning, 65
Liar: merged with Do-evil, 25; con-
    trasted with Lady Meed, 66; har-
    bored by pardoners, 71, 89; in
    league with spicers, 94; harbored
    by minstrels, 98; censured by
    King, 116–17
-liche, 35, 36, 40, 52, 126